Marked for Life

Peace?

Richard Deats

Olive Teller

Marked for Life
The Story of Hildegard Goss-Mayr

Richard Deats

Foreword by Mairead Corrigan Maguire

New City Press
Hyde Park, New York

Published in the United States by New City Press
202 Cardinal Rd., Hyde Park, NY 12538
www.newcitypress.com
©2009 Richard Deats

Cover design by Leandro de Leon

Library of Congress Cataloging-in-Publication Data:

Deats, Richard L., 1932-
   Marked for life : the story of Hildegard Goss-Mayr / Richard Deats.
      p. cm.
   Includes bibliographical references.
   ISBN 978-1-56548-309-5 (pbk. : alk. paper) 1. Goss-Mayr, Hildegard. 2. Catholics—
Biography. 3. Nonviolence—Religious aspects—Christianity. I. Title.
   BX4705.G6174645D43 2008
   282.092—dc22
   [B]   2008034424

Printed in the United States of America

Dedicated to
the memory of

Jean Goss

husband and life partner of Hildegard
who shared her passion and vision for
building a nonviolent world

Contents

Articles by
Hildegard Goss-Mayr

Foreword

In reading Richard Deats' compelling account of the truly astonishing life of Hildegard Goss-Mayr, I am filled with a sense of the magnificence of the human person when transformed into compassion and love through the gifts of the Holy Spirit. No task is too much, no place too far to travel, no one in whom the person of God is not seen and served, such is the kindness and generosity of Hildegard Goss-Mayr, and we are all touched and grateful for such a soul force in our world.

There is much talk today about our interconnected and interdependent world and the need for us to deepen our sense of world family and responsibility to each other and the earth. Hildegard Goss-Mayr and her life's companion, Jean Goss, were over half a century ago in the mid '40s speaking such a language of universality and love of humanity, but not only speaking the language, they were moving around the world, carrying out their active nonviolent service to humanity — especially to the poorest of the poor.

How small the world feels when you read this beautiful book about Hildegard written by her dear friend, Rev. Richard Deats. It seems there was no corner of it too far to go for her to spend time to listen and learn from others, to share the message of Jesus' nonviolent love, of peace and reconciliation. Everywhere she went she joined in solidarity with people of all faiths, and none, sharing their belief and truth that killing is not in the spirit of true love, that all faiths can join together in spreading this truth, that every human life is sacred and the spirit of God lives in all men and women.

As a young woman growing up in a deeply committed Catholic family, Hildegard's faith found deep roots in the gospel of nonviolent love and service. Her parents' example of reaching out in forgiveness and love to everyone, especially the enemy (if they believed in such a concept as when love becomes so deep, there is no such thing as an enemy) but they lived under Nazi occupation and had to make choices to love or not to love. As a young woman Hildegard chose the path of love and through her prayer life came into absolute nonviolence — a gift from God to all truthseekers who knock on God's door and receive in abundance.

Hildegard was blessed abundantly: the gift of faith; the gift of love of her life's partner, Jean Goss; their twins, Etienne and Myriam; friends all around the world; and much, much more. Having received much, she gave much, including her life in the service of God and the world. I am sure this call to service was many times very hard for Hildegard. To leave her children and travel to strange and often dangerous countries, often alone, must often have caused her tears and fear, but she found strength and courage in her prayers and in the love returned from all who had the gift of her presence.

I had the pleasure of meeting Hildegard and Jean in 1988 when they visited Northern Ireland which was in the midst of violent ethnic/political conflict. It was a dangerous time to come but they did so with great enthusiasm and generosity of spirit. They addressed many groups, visited political and spiritual leaders, gave seminars on nonviolence. They brought us hope and planted many seeds of nonviolence and peace.

Hildegard's great passion was in offering active nonviolence as a way of life, and a creative alternative to armed struggle, militarism and injustice. There were many skeptics to say nonviolence was weak and wouldn't work and that only violence gets results. Hildegard and Jean were steadfast in pointing to the Christian gospels, the Sermon on the Mount, the nonviolent Jesus. They challenged the Christian Churches to teach the nonviolent message of Jesus. But perhaps the greatest witness to this message was in her own presence. Hildegard's gentleness and quiet presence brought peace and calmness to all and to those with whom she disagreed there was a deep respect and reverence for their point of view. Difference, in any form, was not a threat or cause for anger or aggression. You knew that Hildegard could talk about peace because she had become peace. In leading such an active life, traveling the world to teach nonviolence, it must have been always a challenge for Hildegard to find the balance in her life between prayer and action. Yet she models for us the importance of doing so. I am sure it is her life of prayer and contemplation that gives her the inner strength to keep going and giving of herself with love. I see her as a mystic (like Hildegard of Bingen) spending much time in prayer and contemplation and being filled up by the Spirit to go down the mountainside and into the offices of Government and Church Palaces to plead against militarism and war, and into the slums to serve the person of Jesus in all she meets. To me Hildegard is living proof that there are many spiritual paths to God and whilst some of the mystics live on the mountain and in the monasteries, there are also the active mystics all around us doing God's work, quietly, with humility, gentleness and joy.

Deo Gratias for the life of Hildegard. And also for the life of her beloved partner and co-worker for nonviolence, Jean Goss who in 1991 passed to Heaven to be with the God he loved and served so faithfully all his life.

Mairead Corrigan Maguire
www.peacepeople.com

Mairead Corrigan Maguire was awarded the Nobel Peace Prize in 1976 for her leadership in the peace movement of war-torn Northern Ireland. Co-Founder of Peace People of Northern Ireland, she has, since the 1970s, become a worldwide ambassador for peace.

Preface

Hildegard Goss-Mayr is one of the preeminent teachers of nonviolence in our time. A pioneer teacher and visionary, she has helped forge a new path for humanity,

The twentieth century, in which the destructive potential of mass killing and war was made possible through military technology, was the most destructive in human history.

At the same time, however, there emerged in the twentieth century another current of thought and action. If humanity demonstrated its lethal potential, it also surprisingly demonstrated its capacity for carrying out not only individual deeds of exceptional goodness but the capacity for building transformative and hope-engendering nonviolent mass movements. This arose in large part due to the life and witness of Mohandas Gandhi and the freedom struggle in India. This movement was built on the philosophy and practice of *satyagraha*, truth force. Gandhi taught and demonstrated that the decisive and enduring power in the affairs of persons and nations is nonviolence. Slowly humanity is learning this truth.

Following the Gandhian movement that nonviolently overcame the British Raj, at the time the world's mightiest empire, in country after country and place after place — the southern United States, the Philippines, South Africa, much of Latin America and the Soviet bloc, et al. — violent structures and practices were toppled for the most part by nonviolent means.

This nonviolent groundswell stimulated key figures of the world's religions to re-examine faith's relationship to violence and to see afresh the life-affirming nature of religion. Absolute respect for the human being, shalom, salaam, compassion: these concepts are the building blocs of peace and harmony, among all people, with nature and with the divine reality underlying all of life. These are not just personal but social as well.

Hildegard Goss-Mayr emerged from World War II determined to give herself to the vocation of peace so that from the ashes of war would be built a hopeful, nonviolent future for humanity. A theologian, an activist, and a practical mystic, for over half a century and on every continent she has written and spoken and taught the way of peace and active nonviolence. Her place in history will grow as her seminal role in constructing a peaceful future is discovered.

I have been privileged to know Hildegard as a friend and colleague for over thirty years. Together we have carried out nonviolence workshops and participated in conferences in the Philippines, South Korea, Hong Kong, Bangladesh, and Russia. We have worked together in Israel and Palestine, Germany, Austria, France and Holland. We taught a five-day seminar on "The Gospel and Active Nonviolence" at Maryknoll (New York), sponsored by the Maryknoll Sisters and the Overseas Ministries Study Center (New Haven).

Over many years I have kept extensive files of her articles, talks, reports and letters, which with her books convey her life and work. I am particularly indebted to the account of her life and work as carefully recorded in her last book, *Wie Feinde Freunde Werden.* I am also grateful for the many emails and extended phone conversations we have had during the writing of this book. She has been unfailingly accessible and helpful.

I am indebted to insights and help given by Hildegard's sister, Elly, her husband Robert Nagler and Hildergard and Jean's children, Etienne and Myriam; and to Dom Hélder Câmara, Cardinal Sin, President Aquino, Andre Gregorczyck, Fr. Alfred Bour, Adolfo Perez Esquivel, and Sr. Marlene-Karla. Translations of various articles and letters were provided by Francois de'Heurl (sadly recently deceased), Justus Vogel, John Lindsay Poland and John Leys. Photos and other assistance were provided by Peter Hammerle, Gregory Kennnedy-Salemi, Doug Hostetter, Jim Forest and Stan Morris. Special encouragement was given by my wife Jan, and by Janet Chisholm, John Dear and the staff of New City Press. Any errors and shortcomings are due solely to me.

Unless otherwise noted, biblical passages come from the Revised Standard Version.

This biography is my humble effort to help Hildegard's life reach and inform the wider audience her life and work deserve.

Richard Deats
Nyack, New York

Introduction

In 1942, amidst the war sweeping across Europe and much of the world, Adolph Hitler triumphantly entered Vienna, capital of the Austrian state that the Third Reich had now swallowed up.

Schools had been dismissed so that students could join the throngs that had gathered along the Ringstrasse, the central boulevard of the city. Adulation swept over the crowd as Hitler rode by, standing in his official black car. "Heil, Hitler!" they shouted, raising their right arms in salute.

Among the school children stood a twelve-year-old girl, Hildegard Mayr, the daughter of Catholic pacifist parents. Her family, especially her father Kaspar, had been under surveillance and harassment as the Nazis tightened their control over Austria and sought to snuff out any signs of disloyalty to the new order. Kaspar Mayr had lost his job in Catholic and ecumenical peace work and was barred from the chamber of writers.

Hildegard had witnessed the violence spreading over the city. Jews, pacifists and communists were being questioned, many losing their work and property, growing numbers killed with others rounded up and shipped off to internment camps. The occupying German army and the swastika were evident everywhere.

As Hildegard saw her classmates join the crowd's hysteria, she sensed as never before the power of evil. Refusing to salute, she stood fast, holding her arms to her side. She later wrote, "I felt a huge force pressing on me, which swept everyone away, and I said to myself, 'you have to resist, you can't let yourself be caught up, don't raise your hand even if they lynch you!' "

This experience would remain with Hildegard, an indelible reminder that no matter what she must resist evil and remain faithful to the God of peace. She says she was "marked for life."

After the war, Hildegard prepared herself for a peace vocation. In the coming years, she and her husband, Jean Goss, worked all over the world, and came to be recognized for their pioneering efforts for peace in nations on every continent.

This is Hildegard's story.

1
The Early Years in Vienna

Kaspar Mayr, one of ten children, was born to a family of devout Catholic farmers in Upper Bavaria, near the Austrian border. Even while young he was inspired by the Christian vision of goodness and peace. At the age of ten he was sent to a seminary in Munich where he developed an interest in philosophy and theology. His studies were interrupted during World War I when he was drafted into the German army. At Verdun, he witnessed the horrible carnage of hundreds of thousands killed in trench warfare. Captured by the French, he became a prisoner of war. These brutal experiences deepened his faith and convinced him to become a pacifist, especially influenced by the friendship and teachings of Father Max Josef Metzger, founder of a peace community in Graz (in southern Austria), Christ the King Society of the White Cross.

After his release in 1921, Mayr became active in the work of the Society of the White Cross, where he met his future wife, Erika. He went on to lead Catholic International, another peace endeavor Metzger founded. After they married in 1923, the Mayrs moved to Switzerland when the office of Catholic International moved there. Then in 1926 they transferred to London when Kaspar was hired by the International Fellowship of Reconciliation (IFOR), a growing ecumenical nonviolent movement. Metzger and Mayr were among the first Catholics to join IFOR, a witness for which they paid dearly. During World War II, Mayr suffered under the Nazis but was able to continue his work clandestinely. Metzger, however, was martyred (Goss-Mayr, *Wie Feinde* 15[1]).

IFOR had been founded by Christians who felt called to devote themselves to Jesus, the Prince of Peace. Its members believed that they should reject war and follow the way of the cross. In early August, 1914, at Lake Constance in southern Germany an international ecumenical conference convened to head off the looming European war. No one wanted it, yet it drew inexorably closer. Many Christians thought that surely the churches could save Europe from catastrophe. In the midst of the conference, however, Germany invaded Belgium and the 150 participants had to hurry home across a continent that plunged quickly into war. Two of the delegates — Henry Hodgkin, English Quaker, and Friederich Siegmund-Schultze, German Lutheran pastor of the Kaiser — pledged as they departed that even in war Christians are called to nonviolence and reconciliation. As St. Paul had written, "If any man be in Christ, he is a new creation; old things are passed away; behold, all things are become new. And all things are of God who hath reconciled us to Himself by Jesus Christ, and has given to us the ministry of reconciliation" (2 Cor 5: 17–19). Siegmund-Schultze pledged to Hodgkin, "Whatever happens, nothing is changed between us" (Brittain 30). Out of that pledge the Fellowship of Reconciliation was born, a pledge that the devastation and deaths of World War I only intensified.

In 1928 the IFOR office moved to Vienna, which became the Mayr family's permanent home. Vienna, in the heart of Europe between East and West, was a logical place for the international office. From 1928 to 1933 Kaspar Mayr worked with Hermann Hoffman, a priest from Breslau, in the difficult task of German-Polish reconciliation. Germany and Poland had frequently been at war and the period between World I and World War II was marked by severe tensions between the two countries. Mayr and Hoffman were able to get help from the papal nuncios, Cardinal Lauri of Warsaw and Cardinal Pacelli of Berlin, who in 1939 would become

---

1. The source throughout for *Wie Feinde Freunde Werden* by Hildegard Goss-Mayr includes a typed, unpublished translation in English as well as portions translated by the author.

Pope Pius XII. This critical work continued until 1933, when the Nazis' racist ideology that considered Slavs inferior and not deserving of such efforts ended it.

After World War I, the German-speaking areas of the defeated Austro-Hungarian Empire became Austria. As Hildegard observed, "The empire was gone and Austria was just a small country with a big capital." The post-war world economic crisis radicalized workers, leading to partisan civil strife between the left and the right. The First Republic of Austria lasted from 1918 to 1934, when Egelbert Dolfuss of the Christian Social Party, chancellor since 1921, was assassinated by pro-Nazi elements that wanted unification with Germany. Although only four at the time of the assassination, Hildegard recalls standing on the veranda of their home and seeing airplanes flying over. The five Mayr children grew up in a household filled with discussions about the events such as the chancellor's assassination and the Japanese-Chinese war, which they would act out. On one occasion, the children burned up a doll dressed in an SS uniform, although they made sure their father didn't know about it!

On March 12, 1938, the Anschluss, the Nazi occupation of Austria, began. Although forbidden by the Treaty of Versailles, a referendum to unify Austria with Germany received almost unanimous support in April. Hence, from 1938 to 1945 an independent Austria was integrated into the Third Reich.

After Hitler came to power in 1933, the Mayr family faced new difficulties. While traveling in Germany, Kaspar's travel documents were confiscated. The IFOR office was forced to move to Paris, and Kaspar, an outspoken and well-known pacifist, was removed from the Chamber for Literature, the instrument of the Nazi regime that controlled all publications and authors. For a while he was permitted to write at the Vienna Pastoral Institute, but this work, too, was eventually prohibited.

The Mayrs opened their home to visitors from other countries, especially Christian young people and religious socialists. Hildegard and her brothers and sisters experienced first-hand the warmth and joy of such a home, but growing Nazi control increased the family's strictures and privations. Sensing what was coming, Kaspar burned many of his papers. He acted just in time. As he had feared, the Gestapo raided the home and ransacked his study, confiscating "subversive" literature and correspondence. Much of Kaspar's international correspondence was spared when Hildegard's mother offered the Gestapo agents liquor, which they drank while sitting on the trunk where the letters were hidden! They left, but kept the Mayr home under careful surveillance.

In the subsequent months and years, Kaspar earned only a small income through his unofficial translation work. He became very ill as the persecution grew, following the outbreak of World War II in September 1939 (Goss-Mayr, *Wie Feinde* 14–17).

Many of Austria's 200,000 Jews were either killed outright or shipped off to the extermination camps. Communists, socialists and progressive Catholics were also persecuted or killed, as were homosexuals, Jehovah's Witnesses, Gypsies, and members of the anti-Nazi student group, the White Rose. The two most well-known Austrian Catholic martyrs were the peasant Franz Jägerstätter, executed in 1943, and Kaspar's mentor in pacifism, Father Max Joseph Metzger, executed in 1944. Their "crimes" were identical: as pacifist Christians, they supported human rights and opposed war, refusing to serve in the army or support the Nazi cause. Jägerstätter put it well: "… it is still best if I speak the truth even if it costs me my life." [2] Although branded at the time as a traitor by many of his countrymen, his clear fidelity to Christ and the courage and purity of his sacrifice led to his beatification by the Roman Catholic Church half a century later.

---

2. His 94-year-old widow Franziska and his four daughters, Hildegard, Maria, Aloisia and Rosalia attended the ceremony in Linz, Austria on October 26, 2007.

2
The War and Its Aftermath

Hildegard, the fourth of the five Mayr children, was born in 1930; she was eight at the time of the Anschluss. She and her siblings understood full well the changes taking place which were reflected in family discussions, in their studies, and in their outlook. Daily prayers reinforced the family's spiritual depth.

The whole family took a particular interest in Eastern Europe and in the Eastern Churches. Richard, the eldest of the children, wanted to be a Benedictine priest and work with the Eastern rite churches. At age six, he even started learning Russian from Kaspar's secretary, who spoke Russian and helped teach him.

The mother, Erika, anchored the family as they were swept up in the tumult of the time. With Kaspar's arrest, persecution and subsequent illness, she provided the stability and love that held them together. She had a sunny disposition and planned activities and projects for the children. From their home on a hill in the outskirts of Vienna, Kaspar, when he was able, enjoyed taking the children on long walks in the woods. Hildegard's older sister, Elly, remembers their father playing funny games with the children, as well as teaching them about the harrowing events of the time in the light of Christian faith. Professor Lester Kurtz of the University of Texas describes the Mayr home as "a pacifist oasis in a desert of violence."

When Hildegard was twelve, all the school children went to the main thoroughfare, the Ringstrasse, to see the Führer and his soldiers pass by. With great fervor and excitement the people raised their arms in the Nazi salute, shouting "Heil, Hitler!" Many of these children, caught up in adoration of the Führer and intoxicated with the flags and uniforms and military might, would become fodder for the war machine of the Third Reich as members of the Hitler Youth and the League of German Maidens. Hildegard, however, in a brave and dangerous act of defiance, held her arms by her side, refusing to salute. Even at her young age, she knew she was in the presence of evil and summoned up the strength to resist it. This created an indelible impression on her. She says, looking back, "At the time I didn't realize its importance but that experience has marked my life" (Goss-Mayr, *Wie Feinde* 16ff).

The war made food and other essentials scarce. People thought that Vienna would be spared, but in September 1944 heavy Allied bombing started. Some of the neighbors who came out to watch were killed by the blasts. In one raid a 550 lb. bomb landed in the Mayr garden but didn't explode. If it had, the house would have been demolished.

The Mayr children lived in two worlds, carefully watching what they said and did. They could not trust their neighbors, some of whom reported to the Gestapo that the Mayrs were hosting visitors. They had to be very careful at school, knowing that their words might be used to incriminate their father. The fact that he did not work convinced the pro-Nazi teachers that he was at least politically unreliable, perhaps a traitor. One stern teacher made Hildegard sit at the back of the room and treated her harshly. Hildegard was fortunate to have as friends a group of strong girls who drew strength from each other.

Hildegard considers it a miracle that her father was never sent to a concentration camp. Their parents taught them that they had two responsibilities. First, they must support those who opposed the Nazi regime and fascism. Second, they must witness to the alternative way of life by not hating the enemy and by standing for truth and love so that those who sided with the Nazis would experience the meaning of shalom. She recalls that their father taught them "the oneness of all humanity. This oneness ... is God's vision of us, but it cannot come into existence unless we live it. It was very difficult for us to live this but it was the task he gave us — not to hate our colleagues or fellow students who were fascists, but to try to give a witness to them."

(Goss-Mayr, *Wie Feinde* 17). This extraordinary stance was rare, especially in wartime and under totalitarian military occupation.

In the summer of 1944, because of the bombing of Vienna, all school children up to the age of 15 were evacuated, often to Nazi camps. In one bright spot for the family, three of the Mayr children were allowed to go to their uncle's farm in nearby rural Bavaria. Because they would be in "the Fatherland," the authorities considered it safe enough and allowed them to go. Kaspar and Erika, with one of their daughters, decided to remain at home in Vienna. Richard, the eldest, was conscripted into the German army, later to die on the Russian front. The children thrived in the beauty of the countryside with its open air, sunshine, and fresh produce. The friendly surroundings offered a respite from wartime life in the city. Although it was illegal, they listened to the BBC. A priest who had been released from prison helped teach the children, giving some degree of normalcy to their lives. As the war wound down, growing numbers of displaced soldiers and refugees flooded Bavaria. They received food and other help from this generous farm family.

Every day, Hildegard and her siblings saw bombers overhead and did not know if their family in Vienna was still alive. Communication was difficult at best. Widespread destruction and censorship only heightened Kaspar and Erika's isolation and foreboding. In April 1945, however, the Russian army arrived and on May 8 the war ended. A priest brought news to the Mayr children on the farm that their parents had survived. After years of unspeakable destruction and death, the nightmare finally ended. What would follow was the new unknown (Goss-Mayr, *Wie Feinde* 17ff).

The Viennese welcomed their Soviet liberators with a mixture of joy and trepidation. Occupying armies can destroy, rape and pillage. When the Red Army reached their neighborhood, Kaspar Mayr and his family acted out of their faith rather than out of their fear. Instead of hiding as the soldiers approached, Kaspar stood at the door and welcomed them. The surprised soldiers eventually put down their guns, removed their hats and coats, and came in. Kaspar introduced them to his wife, son and daughter. When they noticed Richard's photograph on the piano, Kaspar told them how he had died in the war in Russia. On the wall hung an icon of Mary and Jesus that Richard had managed to rescue from a burning house. After his death, the icon was sent home with his other effects. The soldiers recognized it, and some crossed themselves. They shared some of their rations with their emaciated yet cordial hosts. When they left, the soldiers were invited back to this "enemy" household that lived with a different reality (Lester).

Films and books about World War II emphasize its violence and destruction, the necessity to kill or be killed. They praise those who resisted evil but rarely examine the means used to do so. The Mayr family is but one example of another approach and tradition in resisting evil that showed itself here and there across Europe, redemptive sparks of self-giving love. Norwegian teachers refused to teach Aryanized education, even when they were sent to camps in the Arctic. Danish citizens helped their Jewish neighbors escape to Sweden, saving them from certain death in concentration camps. French villagers in LeChambon hid Jewish children in their farms and homes. Berlin pastors helped people being pursued by the Gestapo escape to safety. The Mayrs are part of this tradition of overcoming evil with good.

In October 1945, Hildegard and her siblings returned to Vienna on a train full of evacuees. They had been waiting since May for the Austrian-German border to be re-established and to secure permission and transport. Austria, once again an independent nation, was divided into four zones of Allied occupation — Russian, French, British and American. In 1955 the occupation ended and Austria wrote "everlasting neutrality" into its Constitution, an extraordinary achievement during the Cold War, when Europe and much of the world found itself divided between East and West, communist and capitalist.

The post World War II era proved difficult for young people who had grown up during years of violence, privation, fear and death, with destroyed countryside, bombed out cities, shattered families and communities, interrupted home life, postponed schooling, and abnormal everyday life. Hildegard speaks of her depression during the aftermath of the war. Like so many other young survivors, she bore wounds within. She had to face not only the shattered life of Austria and indeed the entire continent, but she had to struggle with the inner despair created by frightening wartime experiences. Looking back on the war, Hildegard wrote:

> In 1944 ... I was a fourteen-year-old girl, sitting in a shelter, trapped, waiting for the bombs of the Allied Forces to kill me. What does it do to the mind, to the heart, to the soul of a human being confronted in this way with violent death? Does it not destroy your confidence in life, your faith in the goodness of humans? Such a situation forces you to take a basic decision: either to submit to the forces of death, of bitterness, hatred and the spirit of revenge — or to reject violence radically and to seek the forces of life that are able to overcome evil at its root in the minds and hearts of human beings as well as in the structures of society. It was out of this experience that the conviction grew in me that I could not go on living unless I dedicated my life to peacemaking through the power of nonviolence. Later I found in the message of the universal self-giving love of Jesus the inspiration for this path. It has nourished and enlightened my whole life and witness. (Goss-Mayr, *Wie Feinde* 17)

As normalcy began to return, formerly closed opportunities opened. In 1948, Hildegard and her brother Norbert attended an International Youth Conference in England organized by the British FOR. There they met others of their generation from various European countries, all seeking to put their lives back together and find their place in the post-war world.

Little by little Hildegard drew upon her upbringing in a household with humane, universal values and commitments to begin to discover her vocation. At the age of eighteen, she began a five-year program of studies in philosophy, philology and history at the University of Vienna. In her second year (1949–50) she attended Albertus Magnus College in New Haven, Connecticut, in a post-war program for German and Austrian exchange students to study democracy. Because of the quality of her academic work, she was put into the senior year. In her thesis she contrasted romantic and realistic views concerning "The Small Town in American Literature, 1865–1930." In 1953, at the end of her fifth year at the University of Vienna, she received, with a Gold Medal, a doctorate in philosophy *sub auspiciis praesidentis*. Presented to her by the President of the Republic, this was the first time this highest degree was awarded to a woman. She felt fortunate that her gender did not impede her academic achievements (Goss-Mayr, *Wie Feinde* 17).

3

Beginning the Work
of Reconciliation

Hildegard finished her studies with a strong calling to work for
peace. Following the violence of World War II came the fierce
antagonisms of the Cold War between East and West. Renewed international suspicions and a new arms race — which the development of nuclear weapons made more dangerous than ever —
convinced Hildegard of the critical need for the work of reconciliation. Militarism again became predominant, as NATO in the West
and the Warsaw Pact in the East prepared to resist each other's at-
tacks. Fearing the atomic weapons of the United States, the Soviet
Union developed its own nuclear capability. Fear of a new global
conflict burgeoned; some speculated that a new war might bring
about the end of civilization.

The ideological divide between East and West inhibited normal
international, national, and religious relationships. Travel and trade,
understanding and cooperation became strained and often impossible. In the West people who reached out to the East were labeled
"Communists"; those in the East who reached out to the West were
labeled "traitors." To speak of peace and disarmament aroused
charges of treason. Even in the churches — Catholic, Orthodox and
Protestant — many succumbed to these attitudes, using religion to
justify their national and ideological attitudes and policies, including
the possibility of yet another war.

Following the end of World War II, the international office of the
Fellowship of Reconciliation had been re-established, and in 1953

the IFOR secretariat asked Hildegard to join its staff. Her youth, intelligence, experience and faith appealed to them. With the invitation, Quaker theologian, IFOR and ecumenical leader Douglas Steere wrote to her, "Give prayerful thought to all your projects, so that you will remain protected and inspired by God's power, because it is only through this power that we can have permanent influence and pass it on to others" (Goss-Mayr, *Wie Feinde* 19). The offer allowed her to focus her work on peoples not only recovering from World War II, but now facing new threats and dangers. Having grown up in a peace family and living in a neutral country located on the divide between East and West, she decided she was uniquely prepared to help build bridges between the two hostile sides.

Austria had a strong peace tradition. Austrian novelist Baroness Bertha von Suttner, first woman to win the Nobel Peace Prize (1905), had a strong influence on her friend Alfred Nobel. She worked with the Jewish pacifist and journalist Alfred Fried, recipient of the 1911 Nobel Peace Prize. For his refusal to serve in Hitler's army, Austrian peasant and pacifist Franz Jägerstätter was martyred. Hildegard's nationality, her life experience, academic training (including fluency in German, English and French), combined with the ability to travel between the two blocs made her ideally suited for this work. She believed God was leading her to a life-long vocation. Jesus Christ, the Prince of Peace, spoke to her inmost beliefs and feelings.

Her father revived his East-West work and with it renewed contacts with persons committed to reconciliation on both sides. Kaspar Mayr began publishing the periodical *Der Christ in der Welt*, which helped build and deepen the Christian (especially the Catholic) understanding of and commitment to the nonviolence of the Gospel. It provided a forum for Catholic intellectuals such as Reinhold Schneider, Friedrich Heer, Pierre Lorson, Pie Regamey, Thomas Merton and Dorothy Day.

In the early centuries the Church followed the nonviolence of Jesus. Christians refused ultimate allegiance to the Roman emperor, even when such a stand led to martyrdom. They would not serve in Roman Legions. But in the fourth century, when

Constantine accepted Christianity himself and made it the official religion of the empire, things changed. Now, no one could join the army unless he were Christian. The Church's roots sank deeply in Roman culture and it became a staunch defender of the empire. The doctrine of the just war replaced the pacifism of the early Church, with the nonviolent Gospel proclaimed and lived only in certain monastic communities and by some devout clergy, nuns, and laypersons. After the Reformation, most Protestant churches also accepted the just war tradition. Reformation, however, also gave rise to the historic peace churches in the Mennonite, Quaker and Brethren pacifist traditions.

By the twentieth century, with its devastating wars arising out of totalitarianism, militarism and extreme nationalism, the doctrine of just war came under increasing scrutiny in the churches. As it advanced, military technology made war ever more lethal, its destructiveness ever more difficult to contain. More and more innocent people were killed, cities and the countryside laid waste. Consequently individuals and certain groups within the churches began to re-examine and re-discover the pacifism of the early church and its roots in the teaching of the nonviolent Jesus.[1]

Building upon her pacifist heritage, Hildegard established three aspects of her work:

1. the development of East-West dialogue as contacts were built and friendships were established, grounded in both sides genuinely speaking the Truth;
2. advocacy of nonviolence and conscientious objection, concepts that at the time both sides largely discounted; and
3. establishing contacts with the churches, which had been shut off from one another during World War II and the subsequent Cold War.

International conferences brought together disparate voices who shared the gospel's message to follow Jesus Christ, who transcended

---

1. Eileen Egan describes these developments in detail in her *Peace Be With You. Justified Warfare or the Way of Nonviolence* (Maryknoll, NY: Orbis Books, 1999).

East and West, Communist and Capitalist, Catholic, Protestant and Orthodox. These unofficial conferences were grounded in a belief in reconciliation, genuine dialogue, and the willingness to reach out to churches and human rights organizations, as well as to communists and communist organizations. The right of conscientious objection from military service was integral to this work, as well as the need for a deep spirituality.

The first of these conferences, held in Vienna in 1958, was ground-breaking in its breadth, especially during a time of mutual suspicion and separation. The conference included two Russian Orthodox priests, a Polish priest, an Austrian theologian and various Protestant theologians such as Hannes de Graaf of Belgium. The Archbishop of Vienna, Franz König (named Cardinal by Pope John XXIII in 1958), supported such initiatives. During his long, influential life, he remained a close friend and ally of the Goss-Mayrs (Goss-Mayr, *Wie Feinde* 20–24).

Those who did not live through this time may not find these principles and meetings remarkable, but in those harsh and suspicious post-war days, they were all too rare and difficult to put into practice. Hildegard's strong faith and courage, combined with her intellectual depth, were key to the importance of the conferences.

During this bridge-building work and witness, Hildegard met the Frenchman Jean Goss in Paris in 1954.

4

Jean Goss, Partner for Life

Jean Goss grew up and lived in a way that could not have differed more from Hildegard's. His French family moved frequently and lived on the edge financially. His father abandoned his five children, leaving their mother to provide for them. Despite the family's poverty she took care of her children with ample love.

Jean attended public schools but as the second eldest, he had to go to work early as an unskilled laborer. He joined a labor union when he was only fifteen and became involved in a strike of the French railway which led to the fall of the government. He learned the strength of unions that struggled for justice without weapons, building solidarity and unity.

When Hitler rose to power and war engulfed France, Jean enlisted in the army, fought fiercely, and became a highly decorated soldier. Yet he experienced a great interior struggle. He came to realize that he was not killing Hitler, but other ordinary men like himself and his comrades. This struggle led him to awaken on Easter in 1940 with the awareness of an enormous and unconditional love for humanity, including the enemy he was expected to kill. Alfred Bour, French priest and friend, says that Jean received "the nonviolence of God in one night, like a stream of light." Bour also notes that "… fire is the best symbol for Jean Goss — light and warmth without borders" (Deats 13). He found great happiness and confidence in this awakening, even though at that moment the Nazis captured him. Even as a prisoner, Jean's revolutionary conversion experience continued. He had difficulty ex-

pressing such overwhelming love, so he would go out into the
woods and shout songs and praise to God. Some thought he must
be going mad. Jean would later put it this way:

> Christ revealed Himself to me not as an idea, not as an
> ideology or doctrine or religion. He revealed himself to me
> as something I knew very well — as a human being. I found
> the very human being my soul had been seeking , the person
> who loves all people without exception — the good and
> bad, workers and bosses, believers and unbelievers, the
> exploited and oppressors, because they were all created
> by God in love ... this love is active and dynamic and
> aggressive against evil and injustice but never against hu-
> man beings! It is life-bringing, always and everywhere.
> (Goss-Mayr, *Wie Feinde* 10)

Jean spoke of his faith to the fellow prisoners and found that when
he genuinely and courageously loved, even Marxists and atheists
saw the truth in his witness. One fellow prisoner, a Communist, ini-
tially made fun of him, challenged him and strengthened him to such
a degree that Jean found he could witness even to a member of the SS.

Eventually a group of prisoners joined Jean in trying to practice
absolute love. Word of its transforming effect spread to other
camps. Once Jean was tortured and sentenced to death. Before the
execution, he spoke of the joy he felt in knowing that he would
soon be united with the God of Love. Jean told the officer about to
shoot that God loves him completely and that he did, too. He said
that this love is possible only because it is Jesus, not he, who is
all-loving. The executioner lowered his revolver. For disobeying
orders, he was arrested and taken away. Jean never saw him again
and did not know what happened to him.

After the war, Jean returned to his family, now committed to
living a life of simplicity and poverty. They were shocked at the
radical love that led him to befriend the poor and homeless, even
bringing some of them home. He aligned himself with the worker
priests and their efforts for bettering the lives of the poor. He once

again became active in unions and the ongoing struggle for justice (Goss-Mayr, *Wie Feinde* 8–11).

Jean faced the most difficult problems with religious authorities and institutions whose compromises with wealth, power and violence distanced them from the radical message of Jesus. He talked with many well-known theologians, but even those who said they understood his message rejected it personally. He would even stop priests he chanced upon and ask them if they rejected violence and war.

Jean often found himself isolated from the Christian community where he expected to find his natural allies and friends. The very intensity of his religious experience made him impatient with the more settled life of congregations he visited. Fortunately two persons who understood what he was proclaiming became special friends and colleagues. One of these was Henri Roser, a Reformed Church pastor and leader in the International Fellowship of Reconciliation. Roser shared Jean's commitment to radical love as proclaimed and embodied in Jesus. He helped Jean develop his theology of peace, in the company of others who were following the same path. Through Roser Jean joined the French Fellowship of Reconciliation and in time became its leader.

The second was Anne Boirard, a brilliant humanist, an agnostic, a Socialist intellectual who saw the profound, indeed revolutionary nature of what Jean was saying. She helped him to clarify and deepen his nonviolent message. The Spirit blows where it will and friends and soul mates are often found in surprising and unexpected places.

Jean became part of a committee formed in 1947 working for the recognition of conscientious objection. In 1948 he made a final break with his military past. He returned his military papers and medals to the Minister of Defense, saying that his conscience prohibited him from killing and from anything connected with killing. At that time France did not have a law recognizing conscientious objection and Jean thought that he would be punished for this act. Indeed, in many countries, conscientious objectors were arrested, tried, and sentenced to prison. Even today, many countries still do not recognize conscientious objection as a right. Those who refuse to bear arms are considered cowards and traitors and frequently are jailed. Surprisingly, Jean was not incarcerated. Not until 1963, however, after France's war with Algeria ended, did President Charles de Gaulle accept a new law protecting conscientious objectors.

Jean protested the long, bloody Algerian war and counseled conscientious objectors. When the army sought to draft this combative mystic, Jean responded that he was ready to go to prison. Wherever he was he would proclaim the absolute nature of Christian love. The authorities, impressed by his outstanding military record and by the authenticity of his conversion while a prisoner of war, decided not to compel him to serve (Goss-Mayr, *Wie Feinde* 12–13).

In October 1947 Jean was heartened to read in *L'Osservatore Romano*, the Vatican newspaper, that Monsignor Alfredo Ottaviani (soon to become a Cardinal and head of the Curia's guardian of doctrine, the Congregation of Faith) wrote that "modern warfare substantially contradicts the doctrine of a just war because it allows the mass murder of innocent people, and that it is therefore to be rejected." He argued that it should be replaced with such things as negotiation and the work of international bodies (Goss-Mayr, *Wie Feinde* 13ff).

Jean and several other lay activists subsequently requested an audience with Monsignor Ottaviani. After receiving no answer to their three requests, in 1950 Jean went to Rome alone. Without an official invitation, he was not admitted. Finding the location of Ottaviani's office, however, he dashed across the courtyard and up the stairs. The startled staff grabbed him but he shouted loudly that as a faithful member of the Church he should be allowed to speak to Ottaviani. Just then the Monsignor opened his door to see what was happening. Jean, typically at no loss for words, told him he must speak to him about the great evil of modern war. In their two hour discussion, Jean bore witness to the radical claim of love. At the end of the conversation Ottaviani told him, "God charged you with a message of truth for humanity and for the Church, and one day the Church will respond. You have a mission: go and bear witness, everywhere!"

In the years that followed, Jean's contact with Cardinal Ottaviani made it possible, as chapter 6 will tell, for Jean (and Hildegard) to appeal to the Theological Commission of the Second Vatican Council.

As Hildegard observes, however, this story demonstrates a lesson of evangelical nonviolence: "One must constantly bring this truth before the eyes of the leaders of the Church, even when they remain closed and backward. To love your adversary means to respect his personal convictions, to expect that he is open to being confronted with truth, to trust that God can change his heart and spirit" (Goss-Mayr, *Wie Feinde* 14).

Along the way of Jean's remarkable life, he met Hildegard Mayr, eighteen years his junior. Their lives were a study in contrasts. This passionate Frenchman, a working class veteran of poverty, had served in the army and been a prisoner of war. His life-transforming conversion to the absolute love of God set him on fire spiritually for the rest of his life. Hildegard, on the other hand, was brought up in a stable Austrian Catholic family. She survived the difficult war years and in time found her calling through scholarly endeavor and evolving religious commitment. Yet opposites attract, and these two lives became one in their shared passion for love and peace throughout the world.

They met in 1954 in Paris where Hildegard was organizing a gathering of Catholic pacifists from various Western European countries. Jean introduced her to his large family, then on his old motorcycle took her around Paris to meet members of various renewal movements, including Dominicans, and members of Pax Christi and of the Mouvement de la Reconciliation (MIR), the French Branch of the International Fellowship of Reconciliation. She met Professor Louis Massignon, a pioneer in Muslim-Christian relations; this friendship foreshadowed their future Muslim-Christian work.

She also met members of the worker-priest movement, a mission begun in 1943 and that, in 1945, received the support of the French bishops and the approval of Pope Pius XII. This movement of French priests worked alongside laborers, many of whom had become alienated from the Christian faith. The priests, in their zeal to identify with the poor, had shed their clerical garb and many had joined communist labor unions. Some had even left the priesthood, and some had married. In time the movement fell out of favor with the pope and the bishops until in 1953, all of the worker priests were recalled. Interestingly, John XXIII refused to reinstate the priests but in 1965, Paul VI gave his approval to a revival of this radical experiment in promoting compassion and justice with workers.

Jean and Hildegard grew to love each other and sought to discern how together they could live out their callings to follow the absolute love of the gospel. On meager resources, and with constant travel and complex responsibilities, how could they establish a home and family? For three years they struggled and prayed for clarity as their relationship deepened.

In 1957, IFOR accepted Hildegard's proposal to establish a small center in Vienna for East-West work. At length, Jean came to see that this was the way that they could fulfill their lives and vocational commitments together. It was not easy to leave his city and country, but Jean believed that God had opened this path for him with Hildegard. They celebrated their engagement in Jean's home parish in Arcueil, a Paris suburb. The church was packed, appropriately, with people from every religious persuasion — Catholics, Protestants, atheists — and from the groups with whom Jean had worked for social justice — the poor, the handicapped, veterans, union members. During Easter season they were married in Vienna. Looking back, Hildegard reflects:

> One great gift from Jean for me was his deep unconditional faith in life, which for him, was God. I was able to help make his enthusiastic, for some often overwhelming testimony, understandable, to deepen analyses and to work out projects. Our differences permitted us to complement each other, and we never stopped thanking God for the unique gift of this partnership. It enabled us to have this "impossible" life, a life which led us to all continents but above all enabled us, throughout all our ups and downs, to recognize and love the hidden Christ in our partner, in spite of all weaknesses and imperfections. (Goss-Mayr, *Wie Feinde* 33)

In 1960 Hildegard and Jean had twins — Etienne and Myriam. They grew up in this life experiment in peacemaking, traveling with their parents for extended periods in Latin America — in Brazil (1964–1965) and in Mexico (1970–1971). When they stayed behind in Vienna as their parents traveled, family and a network of friends in the peace movement provided them love and support.

After Jean died, at the Jean Goss Colloquium and Seminar held in Paris (October 30–November 1, 1993), Myriam said, "I always felt my father's immense love. His big heart was always there for me. Our family has tried to live this nonviolent life. Only as an adult have I understood the depth of my father's love."

Jean and Hildegard Goss-Mayr in their early married years

5

Witness in the Cold War

In their first effort together, Jean and Hildegard in 1955 attended a congress marking the tenth anniversary of Pax, a Polish pro-government Catholic group. As in other Eastern European Communist countries, such events and sponsoring organizations served as mouthpieces of governmental policies. Independent meetings and dialogue could take place only around the edges, without official approval. Hildegard knew persons her father had worked with many years earlier, before the war. The post-war situation made maintaining those contacts almost impossible. Three million Poles had died, and the country was devastated by bombing, invasion, combat, and occupation. Because Hitler's policies had been particularly cruel to people he had deemed inferior, such as Poles and Jews, Polish feelings toward German-speakers in general remained raw and bitter.

Nonetheless, toward the end of the congress Hildegard and Jean were able to set up a secret meeting when she had attended Mass at St. Anne's Church and afterwards talked with the priest. She assured him that she did not support the official government line and had come to Poland to witness to the reconciling message of the gospel. The priest was delighted; he knew the work of Kaspar Mayr and took from his breviary a picture of the martyred Fr. Joseph Metzger! This encounter and other contacts led to a clandestine meeting of twenty Christians in an apartment. Doing so was risky, for Poland's Stalinist regime forbade gatherings larger than five. Nonetheless, the invited came to share their thoughts about faith, peace, disarmament and human rights. At the close of the evening, Hildegard and Jean told them that some German Christians, deeply distressed over the Nazi crimes in Poland, desired to personally ask for forgiveness in what they hoped would be a first step to Polish-German reconciliation.

Silence fell over the room. Finally a young writer said, "We love you, Jean and Hildegard. You are the first from the West to come visit us. We are deeply moved by your presence. But what you are asking is impossible! Every stone in Warsaw has been covered by Polish blood due to the Nazi atrocities. We cannot forgive." Once again an uncomfortable silence prevailed.

Hildegard writes, "We insisted: 'Who should make the first step toward forgiveness and reconciliation: those who believe in the God of Love or those who do not know that love?' But the time had not come. Ten years after the war the wounds were still so deep that it was impossible for these Poles to forgive. Therefore on leaving we proposed to recite the prayer that unites all Christians, the Our Father. When we came to the line 'and forgive us our sins as we forgive those who have sinned against us' our Polish friends suddenly broke off, and into the silence the young writer once again spoke: 'Yes, I understand. I cannot be a Christian unless I forgive the Germans' " (Goss-Mayr, *Wie Feinde* 29-31).

A year later, under the leadership of Wladyslaw Gomulka, a more open government replaced Poland's Stalinist regime. This change enabled those Polish Christians to travel to Vienna and meet with German Christians. In the years following they continued to work for German-Polish reconciliation.

The Polish group has lasted to the present day, principally in Warsaw and Krakow. From the Warsaw group came Tadeusz Mazowiecki, whom Lech Walesa would name as Prime Minister in 1987. But the key person was Andrzej Gregorczyk, a brilliant professor of the philosophy of mathematics. In addition to his intellectual skills, he brought a Franciscan attitude of openness, trust, simplicity and good will. He went repeatedly to the Soviet

Union to meet with intellectuals there, and after 1991 to Ukraine in the interest of Ukrainian-Polish reconciliation.[1]

Jean and Hildegard continued their work in Poland, returning often to hold seminars in active nonviolence. They were invited to Gdansk in the period leading up to the founding of Solidarity. The seminar on nonviolent resistance they led there with labor leaders was important in developing the approach of the first independent labor union in the Soviet bloc, a precursor of the vast changes to come in the East.

They made similar efforts to establish contact and understanding in Yugoslavia, Czechoslovakia, Hungary, Romania and Bulgaria. Under precarious conditions Hildegard gave a course in East Germany to Christians who later fostered nonviolent changes in the government. Perhaps the most dramatic of these efforts took place in 1957. Under the auspices of the Communist Young People's Organization of the Soviet Union, a World Youth Festival was held in Moscow. Thirty thousand persons from all over the world were invited to attend — the first opening on such a scale since the Communist revolution of 1917 forty years earlier. Some dismissed it as mere propaganda at the service of world Communism and branded those who accepted the invitation as Communists or at the very least "fellow travelers." Hildegard and Jean, however, welcomed the opportunity to meet and discuss with people on the other side of the ideological divide (Goss-Mayr, *Wie Feinde* 19ff).

In Red Square Jean handed out leaflets in Russian that said, in part:

> Humanity is divided between belligerent groups by the self-ishness of nationalism, by social injustice, by the suppression of individual or collective freedoms, by racism, by hatred, by the politics of force and violence. The only means to lead humanity towards PEACE is the suppression of evil, injustice,

---

1. I was with Andrzej in the 1980s when Solidarity was operating underground. I was part of a Journey of Reconciliation that was meeting people in the Soviet Union and Eastern Europe. Andrzej met us at our hotel for an informative discussion of the current situation. Despite the atmosphere of repression that prevailed at the time, he spoke with great courage, openness, and honesty about what was happening in Poland.

existing oppression which goes against the welfare of the people by the FORCE OF LOVE, TRUTH AND JUSTICE, such as taught and practiced by Jesus Christ in his redemptive life.

Accordingly, we refuse to accept war and its preparation, as well as any murder and any deadly violence, as means to establish and maintain peace. We consider such means to be unworthy of human nature and of man's intellectual and spiritual capacity, and a fatal development towards misery, war, and the total destruction of humanity. (Goss-Mayr, *Wie Feinde* 19f)

Though the police questioned Jean, they allowed him to continue leafleting and discussing at length questions posed from the crowds, questions about peace and war, forgiveness and vengeance, faith and atheism, violence and nonviolence. Such an extraordinary event — a Catholic pacifist publicly involved in a highly charged public discussion in Red Square — had never happened before.

Hildegard and Jean visited Orthodox, Baptist and Catholic churches. They asked the elderly Latvian Catholic priest in Moscow to have a Mass dedicated to world peace during the Festival. They helped him prepare the texts in various languages and then spread word to as many Christians at the Festival as they could.

Ironically, such witness aroused suspicion on both sides. In the West as well as the East, the open search for truth and good will and the support of free conscience were considered subversive. Despite their nonviolent approach to friend and stranger alike, Jean and Hildegard were spied upon and followed. On one trip Jean's briefcase mysteriously disappeared only to just as mysteriously reappear with nothing missing. Sadly, with the crackdown following the Prague spring of 1968, the Goss-Mayrs were refused visas to Czechoslovakia.

In Moscow Hildegard and Jean met Rosa, an actress in the Yiddish theater that had reopened in 1953, after Stalin's death. On their next visit, Rosa set up a dialogue among Jewish intellectuals — from militant Communists to observant Jews. It turned out to be deep and rich, an unforgettable evening.

Chapter 5

Rosa took the Goss-Mayrs to the small wooden house of a Tolstoyan, one of a small group of pacifists who followed the great Russian novelist and pacifist. Retired, this Russian — a Christian anarchist and member of the International Fellowship of Reconciliation — had worked for forty years on cooperative farms. His father, a respected lawyer and Tolstoy's secretary, in the name of Tolstoyans, Baptists, Doukhobors[2] and nonviolent anarchists, had succeeded in bringing to Lenin a 1919 decree granting protection to conscientious objectors. Then, during the changeable early years of the revolution, there were openings that in time would close up. Lenin, as president of the Council of Peoples Commissars, endorsed the decree which read in part:

> We order, upon decision of the People's Tribunal, that any-one who cannot participate in a military service because of religious convictions, should be accorded the right to substi-tute, for the duration of the service required of enlisted persons of the same contingent, a sanitary duty to be served by priority in hospitals for contagious diseases, or another work of public utility, according to his choice.[3]

The Tolstoyan gave Jean and Hildegard a copy of this remark-able yet virtually unknown decree. They in turn brought it to the attention of people not only in the West but in the Communist world (Goss-Mayr, *Wie Feinde* 22–24).

Thus some of the seeds planted in harsh terrain germinated and in time grew to produce remarkable fruits of nonviolent testimony and organizing. Many years later, these fruits in turn contributed to radical change in Eastern Europe and the USSR. They undertook such efforts with a faith that God would provide guidance, soften hearts and open doors.

---

2. A sect sympathetic to Tolstoyan ideals that refused military service, was persecuted by the czarist government and, in 1897, left Russia. The small band of Tolstoyans and more numerous Baptists, however, still saw the Doukhobors as part of the Russian pacifist tradition.

3. I have an English translation of the statement entitled "Decision of the Council of Peoples' Commissars of January 4, 1919 Concerning Exemption from Military Service on Account of Religious Convictions."

6

Peace Lobby at the Second Vatican Council

In the fall of 1962 the world moved to the edge of nuclear war. The doctrine of Mutually Assured Destruction — MAD — accepted by the United States and the Soviet Union came to a showdown over the discovery of Soviet missiles in Cuba. The public confrontation between Nikita Khrushchev and John Kennedy showed the world the potential for catastrophe that Cold War events had brought to humanity. Diplomacy averted war and the world breathed a sigh of relief, even as the continuing danger of conflict remained. Though frail and in declining health, Pope John XXIII encouraged dialogue and negotiation, providing a clear moral dimension neither Eastern nor Western, but universal in its spirit and appeal. He had called for a Second Vatican Council to "open the windows" of the church to the modern world and encourage deep renewal that would manifest itself in addressing the great issues facing the human family, among them the twin scourges of war and nuclear weapons.

During the Council, the pope prepared *Pacem in Terris* ("Peace on Earth," issued April 11, 1963). This encyclical, with its bold call for an end to the arms race and the banning of nuclear weapons, gave hope to people all over the world, to Christians, to the faithful of other religions, to everyone of good will. Departing from the Church's historic distinction between just and unjust wars, John XXIII said that war could no longer be viewed as an instrument of justice. He also made a strong plea for reconciliation and for an end to the harsh Cold

War rhetoric between East and West. He affirmed the nonviolence of the gospel and, flowing from it, the right of conscientious objection to war (Goss-Mayr, *Wie Feinde* 34-36).

Jean and Hildegard, along with other Catholic peace activists, were greatly encouraged by *Pacem in Terris* and various voices for peace emanating from the Vatican Council. An informal but dedicated "peace lobby" formed as a visible presence at the Council, fasting and praying, as well as lobbying the bishops to back the call of the pope and to respond to peace sentiments throughout the world. The "peace lobby" included Eileen Egan and Gordon Zahn of Pax and the Catholic Association for International Peace (CAIP); Lanza del Vasto, his wife Chantrelle and other women from the Community of the Ark in France; Dorothy Day of the Catholic Worker; James Douglass, a young theologian and student in Rome; and the Goss-Mayrs from the International Fellowship of Reconciliation. The Goss-Mayrs, with their many contacts among the hierarchy, made important contributions to the peace lobby's work.

In a convent in the outskirts of Rome, Jean Goss and Jo Pyronnet, Secretary of Action Civique Non-Violente, organized a ten-day fast that highlighted the central importance of both the inner and outward dimensions of the Christian peace witness.

Twenty women from five nations, along with solidarity groups in nine other countries, joined in the fast. In one of the solidarity groups was the Trappist monk, Thomas Merton.

Jean and Hildegard were friends with the influential Cardinal Alfredo Ottaviani, secretary of the Congregation of the Holy Office. Although cautious about many of the proposals for renewal in the church, he strongly supported peace and nonviolence. He advised the Goss-Mayrs to prepare carefully crafted documentation for distribution to the bishops and theologians, many of whom did not question the traditional just war doctrine. The Goss-Mayrs prepared a document that included four major points:

1. modern warfare's indiscriminate destruction of whole populations, leaving the innocent with no escape;
2. the immorality of atomic, bacteriological and chemical weapons, their production and storage, and the threats of their use;

3. the recognition and acceptance of gospel nonviolence as the way to liberation and to overcome aggression, violence and injustice, a recognition that calls for the development of guidelines for effective, nonviolent peace actions;
4. the protection of conscientious objectors to military service, as well as the recognition of the importance of civil disobedience in the face of immoral laws and orders.

This four-fold appeal was sent for comments and corrections to nearly two hundred theologians, priests and laity. The final document was signed by eighty theologians and priests, and three bishops. With the advice of Cardinal König of Vienna and Bishop Dr. Rush of Austria, Pax Christi agreed to propose it to the Theological Preparatory Commission (Goss-Mayr, *Wie Feinde* 36ff).

Cardinal Ottaviani informed Jean and Hildegard when the document had been received and presented to the Commission. He also advised them which bishops and theologians to meet with as an important follow-up. They knew these meetings would be a challenge because of the widespread, well-established acceptance of the principles of just war. In addition, many opposed communism and accepted the necessity of war, even the use of weapons of mass destruction, in dealing with it. The peace lobby faced the contrast between Realpolitik and the Bible, in particular the nonviolence of Jesus.

Jean and Hildegard found their most effective witness in meeting with Commission members not in theological argumentation but in relating their experience in East-West work and in the transformative power of nonviolence and love to break through hostility and overcome evil with good. Once again the Goss-Mayrs demonstrated their extraordinary gift of working steadily and persistently (as the Brazilians would say, *"firmeza permanente"*) for actions consistent with the message of Jesus Christ.

They found an open and receptive attitude in their meetings with the Commission for the Lay Apostolate, where they engaged in a dialogue on the Sermon on the Mount. Likewise, the Secretariat for the Advancement of Christian Unity, led by Cardinal Bea, was very interested in the work for peace the Goss-Mayrs had undertaken among Protestants, Catholics and Orthodox (Goss-Mayr, *Wie Feinde* 23).

The Vatican Council opened on October 11, 1962 amidst great expectations but also apprehensions concerning resistance to the call for renewal. The question of war and peace was not on the original agenda. Jean and Hildegard therefore began rounds of meetings with bishops whom they knew were deeply concerned about this issue and encouraged the effort to present it to the Secretariat for Extraordinary Matters. They convinced key bishops, archbishops and cardinals to support this effort.

A parallel effort by third world bishops sought to get the Council to deal with social and economic injustice and for the church to identify with the poor, an approach that came to be called "the preferential option for the poor." Led by Dom Hélder Câmara of Brazil and others, this effort also succeeded. As a result Cardinal Suenens of Belgium called for the agenda of the Council to deal with the great problems of humanity. From this proposal was born the consideration of the "Constitution on the Church in the Modern World" (*Gaudium et Spes*), thus placing peace and social and economic injustice on the Council's agenda.

Earlier that year Jean and Hildegard had spent four months in Latin America, holding discussions in Brazil with Câmara on the Christian path to liberation. In Rome they found themselves working side by side with him in their parallel efforts to open up the Church.

A special edition of the *Catholic Worker* was prepared for widespread distribution. Its editorial, by Eileen Egan, lifted up the humanity of "the enemy" targeted by nuclear weapons and appealed for a return to the nonviolence of Jesus. Egan "drew attention to Thomas Merton's heart-stopping assertion that 'total nuclear war would be a sin of mankind second only to that of the crucifixion.' It is in order to avoid that great sin that we beg clear words from the Fathers of the Council" (Egan, 174).

In 1963 seventy women peace activists, from many places representing many religious and non-religious traditions and organizations, came to Rome. Inspired and challenged by *Pacem in Terris*, they undertook the Women's Strike for Peace. When they sought an audience with the pope, some on his staff opposed the idea. The women appealed for help to Hildegard and Jean, who knew Cardinal Bea, president of the Secretariat for the Advancement of Christian Unity. Known for promoting wider papal access, he agreed to suggest that John XXIII meet with them. "Good Pope John" said he would address them in his next general audience.

Fulfilling his promise, he told them, "... when you return to your homelands, be ambassadors of peace everywhere: peace with God in the sacredness of consciousness, peace in families, in the workplace, peace with all, as much as it depends on you. This way you will achieve respect and recognition and the blessing of heaven and earth. All of you, be pilgrims of peace!" (*L'Osservatore Romano*, Rome, April 4, 1963, quoted in Goss-Mayr, *Wie Feinde* 35). Not long after this meeting, in June of 1963, John XXIII died. The whole world mourned their beloved Pope John.

The Council continued its work under the newly elected Pope Paul VI. The issue of peace remained under discussion, but mainly from the perspective of natural law rather than from that of Jesus' radical nonviolence. The Goss-Mayrs asked the Council's working group on "the Church in the modern world" that they be allowed to write a brief statement. Their proposal was accepted so they sought theologians who could help them produce it in the language of the Council — Latin. Meeting with the Goss-Mayrs in their small office, Karl Rahner, Yves Congar and Bernhard Häring along with Father Diez-Alegria wrote a statement that focused on the nonviolence of Jesus. Hildegard feels especially indebted to Häring who, she says, "became the greatest moral theologian for nonviolence of the Post-Council era. His burning faith, his profound humanness, the unshakable force of truth and love with which he criticized the Church and challenged her to change filled us with joy and encouragement" (Goss-Mayr, *Wie Feinde* 42).

Once again with Cardinal König's help, they sought the signatures of Cardinals and Bishops from every continent. They succeeded in bringing it before the Council with impressive backing about an issue seen more and more as having world-wide importance. As the Council deliberated about modern warfare, Bishop Boillon of

Verdun, France — where almost a million men were killed or injured in World War I — addressed all those present on October 9, 1965, the last day of the women's fast. Backed by the signatures of seventy bishops, he said:

> Gentleness and humility are admirable qualities of Christ. To practice humility on an international level means that every nation puts a limit to its independence by subordinating itself to an international authority. To practice gentleness on an international level means to reject absolutely the use of weapons. Those who are active in building up nonviolent action and practice it with courage and sacrifice bear witness to this truth.... And since we, honorable Fathers, are talking about war here in the Aula, I wish to inform you that here in Rome a group of twenty women have come together in (total) fasting and prayer, so that the Holy Spirit may enlighten us. Allow me to let these women speak for themselves.

Then, reading from the message of the women, he continued:

> We women know that the council Fathers, who have come together here, will be assuming the terrible responsibility, in the face of the impending threat of death in the world, of taking a stand on the question of war and peace. We have asked ourselves how we, as mothers and protectors of life, can have a part in this fateful decision. Inspired by the words of Paul VI 'to stand up in a vigil watch,' as well as by the penitential encyclical of John XXIII, we are fasting and praying for ten days and imploring God to inspire the Council Fathers with the Gospel's solution which the world is waiting for." (H. Fesquet, *Le Journal du Concile Le Monde*, 1966, 952, quoted in Goss-Mayr, *Wie Feinde* 44)

Supporting Bishop Boillon's address, outside the Aula members of the Community of the Ark had set up the "Foyer Unitas." This exhibit featured Mohandas Gandhi and Martin Luther King, Jr., and the nonviolent movements they led, providing a graphic portrayal of the meaning and transformative power of faith-based nonviolent action.

The efforts of those involved in the "peace lobby" at the Vatican Council succeeded in making plain the inadequacy of the church's traditional stand on "just war," especially in the light of the deadly array of weapons of mass destruction — chemical, biological and nuclear. The immoral character of the mass killings and wholesale destruction of modern warfare in the twentieth century became increasingly clear, even in the face of a strong anti-communist, just war advocacy at the Council by representatives of the Catholic Church in the United States.

With the clear affirmation by Pope John XXIII, supported by the fasting and prayers and witness of the "peace lobby," the nonviolent message of Jesus found resonance and support in many and varied ways at the Council and in its documents. The Council shook loose from is previous consensus concerning the Cold War and the just war theory and took strides in recovering the nonviolence of the early church.

While the breakthrough for which the peace lobby had labored fell short, Hildegard nonetheless found encouragement in the progress that was made. She saw this in *Gaudium et Spes*. For example, section 78 states:

> That earthly peace which arises from love of neighbor symbolizes and results from the peace of Christ which radiates from God the Father. For by the cross the incarnate Son, the prince of peace reconciled all men with God. By thus restoring all men to the unity of one people and one body, He slew hatred in His own flesh; and, after being lifted on high by His resurrection, He poured forth the spirit of love into the hearts of men.... Motivated by this same spirit, we cannot fail to praise those who renounce the use of violence in the vindication of their rights and who resort to methods of defense which are otherwise available to weaker parties too, provided this can be done without injury to the rights and duties of others or of the community itself.

Hildegard says that this is the first time that the Catholic Church affirmed and encouraged the nonviolence of Jesus since the papal

bulls of Honorius III (1221) and Gregory IX (1227), which admon-
ished the Third Order of St. Francis to follow the nonviolence of
Jesus in neither wielding nor even carrying lethal weapons.

Hildegard particularly praises the Benedictine Abbot Christo-
pher Butler of England for addressing thoroughly the rejection of
modern war, saying our oneness in Christ transcends labels such as
Jew or Greek, Eastern Bloc or Western. The Christian's weapons,
says Butler, are not atomic but spiritual. "The gospel does not win
its victories through war but rather by suffering. We do indeed want
to empathize with the difficulties of our statesmen ... but we would
like to add a word to remind you that a good end does not justify immoral means; it also does not justify the conditional intention to
respond to an immoral aggression with forbidden means of defense. Our help will come from the Lord who created heaven and
earth" (Rev. Ch. Butler, O.S.B., "Contributions to the Council on
the Question of War and Peace," in *Der Christ in der Welt* XVI/1,
Vienna, 1966, 17ff, quoted in Goss-Mayr, *Wie Feinde* 45).

Hildegard also praises the call to refuse to obey unjust laws
and commands. Affirming conscientious objection, section 79 of
Gaudium et Spes states "it seems right that laws make humane provi-
sions for the case of those who for reasons of conscience refuse to
bear arms, provided however, that they agree to serve the human
community in some other way."

In assessing the steps of the Council in moving away from
Constantinian Christianity, Hildegard says, "In their struggle for human rights, thousands of Christian witnesses in the Third World have
opposed for years, the repressive, exploiting or racist laws of their
governments and have willingly accepted persecution and even
death for this. They have outdistanced theology, and they live and
fight from the perspective of the Beatitudes" (Goss-Mayr, *Wie
Feinde* 46).

Hildegard refers to Ottaviani's 1947 statement "Bellum omnino
interdicendum" and his reiteration of this at the Council: "Several
Council Fathers have said that war should be completely condemned. I agree completely with this opinion. I would wish that the
schema would speak in greater length about the means of safe-

guarding the continuation of peace and initiatives in this respect.... We have to show the value and importance of the weapons of justice and love."

Finally, *Gaudium et Spes*, section 80, condemns total war: "With these truths in mind, this most holy synod makes its own the condemnations of total war already pronounced by recent popes,[1] and issues the following declaration.

"Any act or war aimed indiscriminately at the destruction of entire cities or extensive areas along with their population is a crime against God and man himself. It merits unequivocal and unhesitating condemnation."

Nonetheless, the Council did not, in the final analysis, condemn the possession of nuclear weapons for the sake of deterrence. Even though the Cold War is now over, the horror of weapons of mass destruction remains, and the threat this poses grows as more and more nations strive to emulate the nuclear states. So, Hildegard says, "... the question arises urgently as to when it will be possible to win over not only the Christian Churches, but all the great world religions to unite together to use moral and political pressure against this threat" (Goss-Mayr, *Wie Feinde* 46f).

Hildegard and Jean Goss-Mayr with Cardinal
Augustin Bea during the Second Vatican Council

---

1. The encyclical refers to Pius XII's allocution of Sept. 30, 1954, his radio message of Dec. 24, 1954, John XXIII's encyclical letter *Pacem in Terris*, and Paul VI's allocution to the United Nations, Oct. 4, 1965.

7

Latin America: From the Just War to *Firmeza Permanente*

In February 1962, the Goss-Mayrs had gone to Latin America to listen and to learn about the situation on that continent. They had been deeply involved in a Europe divided by the Cold War, working for reconciliation, human rights and an end to the arms race. But their global perspective and faith commitment compelled them to participate in the life of the Third World.

Latin America was in ferment. Disparities in wealth, the power of the military, its support by elements in the Catholic Church, and widespread repression led to growing discontent. The successful revolution in Cuba in 1959 had instigated momentum for radical change, violent if necessary, and many progressive religious voices supported it. The church's just war tradition helped foster acceptance of the idea that armed revolution was the wave of the future. Most progressives assumed that nonviolence was merely piecemeal reform, too "soft" for the desperate situation at hand.

Jean and Hildegard had come to observe. Their primary contacts were scattered Fellowship of Reconciliation groups, particularly in Argentina and Uruguay, but they decided to fly first to Bogotá, Colombia. By chance, at the airport they met a Brazilian priest who worked for CELAM, the Latin American Bishops Council. He introduced them to Rev. Camilo Torres, a charismatic sociology professor and chaplain at the state university. Through hours of deep conversations, the Goss-Mayrs learned of his frustration that the upper class and the hierarchy had not awakened to the urgency of the suffering and inequalities in Latin American society, particularly in Colombia. He had decided that violent revolution was the only way forward.

For Torres, Jean contrasted his idealism in going to war so he could kill Hitler and his kind with his experience as a soldier. He explained that the people he killed were not Hitler and the other Nazi leaders but mere conscripts like himself. He said that a revolutionary struggle would kill many of the poor and oppressed but would change little. Systemic change would come not through killing but by living the radical nonviolence of the Gospel.

Torres was intrigued. In all his training for the priesthood, in his study of scripture and in the traditions of the church, he had never encountered this radical nonviolent message. He had studied just war theory and how violence can be justified, but not the relevance of Jesus' actual nonviolent teachings to Latin America's ills. After a time, he asked Jean and Hildegard to stay and work with him and his colleagues. They considered his invitation, but felt they had to continue their journey of listening and learning. Reluctantly, they declined. Shortly later they learned that Torres had joined the guerrillas and was killed in a battle with government troops.

As Jean and Hildegard moved south, at the grass roots level they found amid the great poverty and suffering hopeful signs of change. In their struggle for justice, people were finding power in the literacy methods of Paulo Freire. Peasants and workers had begun to organize. Although since the colonial era the Catholic Church had been aligned with the state and with its military, a liberation theology began to be articulated that stood with the poor and oppressed. The Vatican Council, to begin in October, promised an opportunity to articulate the spirit of change and liberation to ecclesiastical leaders.

For four months of 1962 the Goss-Mayrs listened and observed. They both studied Spanish, funded by Hildegard's lectures in Cuernavaca, Mexico. Their experiences in Latin America deepened the role they would have at the Vatican Council where, with Dom Hélder Câmara and other progressive voices, they witnessed to the role of the church on behalf of the oppressed, the voiceless and the forgotten. Their ongoing discernment and service in the International Fellowship of Reconciliation led them to decide that, building upon their 1962 exploratory trip, they would continue their witness to nonviolent liberation in Latin America.

Many in liberation struggles focused on demanding justice, but the Goss-Mayrs maintained that the method to bring about justice was essential to the outcome being sought. As Gandhi and King taught, the means directly affect the end one seeks and accomplishes. In the process of becoming, the means *are* the end. Hildegard observed:

> Christ came to show that only self-giving love can overcome injustice and its roots in the heart and mind and conscience of the people. If we try to live this out in concrete situations, it means that we must know the situation; we must be with those who suffer and not stand aloof and condemn from the outside; that we must understand that unless we bring this new way into the situation, people will necessarily go into armed resistance because they see no other way. So it is the task of the Christian to show this way in the revolutionary process and this can be done only if the Christian is with the people, with those who suffer, and not above them, but one with them. (Dear)

Jean and Hildegard sympathized with the movement for social revolution, but were convinced, as in the cases of France and Russia, that violence often generates yet another dictatorship, with the new holders of power eliminating their previous allies. The Goss-Mayrs joined Dom Hélder Câmara in speaking of the "endless spiral of violence" in which the poor responded to the violence done to them with yet more violence. Revolutionary violence may arise out of the thirst for justice, but does not change the social structure. Only active nonviolence, which employs peaceful means that generate life, can break the cycle of violence and counter-violence. This transformative approach, which renounces vengeance and domination in all its forms, flows from the gospel.

The struggle was intense. On the one hand, those with power and prestige fought to retain their positions of privilege. On the other, many of the strongest advocates of revolution resisted the call to work nonviolently. Further heightening the stakes, reactionary forces in the United States aligned themselves with those promoting the national security state, reinforcing a status quo in which wealthy and powerful interests predominate. Opponents of such notions of national security were branded as subversive communist elements and forcefully suppressed. States used their military forces to arrest, imprison and torture supporters of democratic movements for change, be they violent or nonviolent.

Building the Movement for Radical Nonviolent Change

Throughout the continent, promoters of nonviolence invited Jean and Hildegard to lead seminars. They worked well together, their differences complementing the impact of their message. Hildegard, quiet and reflective, used careful analysis and winsome appeal. She systematically and comprehensively presented the biblical and philosophical grounds for active nonviolence. Jean, with his French working class origin and experience as a soldier, prisoner of war, and labor organizer, was a more emotional and forceful evangelist of nonviolence. The two of them, gifted storytellers, related the message of nonviolence to historical and contemporary individuals and movements, drawing upon their own experiences during World War II and the subsequent Cold War, especially their work for reconciliation, disarmament and peace in Eastern Europe and the Soviet Union. They combined their own history with their study and support of the Gandhian liberation movement in South Africa and India and the freedom struggle led by Martin Luther King, Jr., in the United States.

In Latin America, they observed grassroots Christian communities awakening to the nature of their oppression and discovering ways to struggle against it, rejecting passive acceptance and mobilizing for social transformation. South Americans were discovering the

Bible's liberating message of "good news to the poor, release to the captives and recovering of sight to the blind" (Lk 4:18).

From Brazil came the term *firmeza permanente* — relentless persistence. This was another expression for what Gandhi called *satyagraha* — Truth Force. Both terms express the dynamic of nonviolent movements throughout the world. Jean and Hildegard grew in their abilities as teachers and facilitators of what, to counter the negative misunderstanding of nonviolence as passive, they most often called *active* nonviolence.

In Montevideo, Uruguay, they struck up an important relationship with the Rev. Earl Smith, a Methodist missionary who led the Fellowship of Reconciliation there. In 1966, he and the Goss-Mayrs collaborated in a consultation, including Protestants and Catholics, with representatives from nineteen countries.

A small but significant movement of radical nonviolence was taking shape. A South American network was being built of peoples' movements struggling against human rights abuses, military oppression, substandard wages and unjust working conditions, environmental degradation, polluted drinking water and lack of access to the land. Bible study and prayer, sealed by the Eucharist, supported and deepened these struggles for justice and peace, bringing people through their sorrows to the resurrection promise of redemptive love, making the broken whole.

The efforts of these scattered small communities met with successes but also with problems, especially governmental opposition and their persecution. To assess the future of the movement, the first continental meeting on nonviolence was held on Pentecost 1971, in Alajuela, Costa Rica — a country without an army, a country that served as a beacon for those working nonviolently towards a better, peaceful future. Representatives from fifteen countries shared their stories of struggle and hope, their problems, and what they had learned in these "experiments with Truth," as Gandhi called nonviolence.

The struggles across the continent, however, even affected Costa Rica. Archbishop Câmara, who had been called "communist" because of his forthright identification with the poor, was invited to join the other bishops, Protestant and Catholic, at the conference. Jean and Hildegard had to convince the Archbishop of San Jose to allow him to come. He was able to attend, but was not permitted to speak. Such was his popularity with the youth, however, that they came to be with him and took him to the university — not as a public speaker, but with permission to answer questions.

The Second Continental Meeting

In 1974 plans began emerging to form a nonviolent liberation movement. Hildegard traveled from country to country, group to group, laying the groundwork for a meeting to be held in Medellin, Colombia.

Ominously, however, the power and reach of dictatorial regimes were growing. Nowhere was this more evident than in Uruguay where all progressives were considered supporters of the Tupamaro guerrilla movement. In Montevideo, Earl Smith's IFOR coordination office was raided repeatedly. Nonetheless Smith announced a public lecture by Hildegard in the Methodist Church. When she arrived, the secret police placed her and the leader of the Fellowship of Reconciliation office under arrest, and questioned them for hours.

Throughout Hildegard sought to remain calm and to show compassion to the officers. Finally, among her papers one of her interrogators discovered letters from her children and photographs of them. The tension broke. When asked about her "party membership" she replied that she did not belong to a party, although her work had "political consequences." He responded by entering on her record, "completamente apolítica" and she was released (Goss-Mayr, *Wie Feinde* 59).

The policewoman transporting Hildegard to the airport for her flight to Buenos Aires produced photos of her own children. When Hildegard reciprocated, the policewoman wept because her country had arrested such a nonviolent person. Again and again, Hildegard's quiet inner assurance had a great impact.

In Buenos Aires she met a young professor of architecture, Adolfo Perez Esquivel, who would become a great gift in promoting nonviolent liberation. Born poor, he identified with the oppressed in their struggles for justice and agreed to come to Medellin. After the military seized power in Argentina, he was arrested and became one of the "desaparecidos," the prisoners who disappeared, few of whom were ever heard of again. But worldwide protests put the government on notice. Human rights groups held vigils at Argentine embassies and missions; letters written on his behalf reached even as far as the Argentine Consulate in New York. The worldwide protests kept Esquivel in the public's awareness and helped pressure the government for his release.[1]

In 1980, Esquivel received the Nobel Peace Prize, further highlighting the radical nonviolent witness in Latin America. Speaking of prisoners like himself he said, "there are only two possibilities of surviving. Either you make a place in your heart for the hate and the violence they are doing to you and hate will become your strength. You survive through hoping that your opponent will be destroyed, so it is in anticipation of his death. This way, you kill twice, once your foe and then yourself. Or you open your heart so much to love that it embraces your torturer; thus you give new life twice, to your enemy and to yourself!" (Goss-Mayr, *Wie Feinde* 67).

Adolfo's wife, Amanda, wrote to Hildegard on November 17, 1980:

> This [Nobel] prize will have to be woven with all those who have been for years in this difficult task of uniting and reconciling brothers. Although I never told you this, through your letters and personal contacts you have stimulated in one way or another the path that Adolfo has walked. He has always had you as his first teacher, who one distant day arrived in Buenos Aires, connected with the Ark and explained in the most simple and humble way what non-

---

1. I participated in the New York City vigils. After Esquivel was freed, he said the worldwide support did much to bring him his freedom and recognition.

violence was … [with] your suggesting … the way to work
and organize. You have always accompanied us in the good
and bad moments. For that reason too, I believe you are also
part of this prize. (Letter from Amanda Esquivel)

Amanda Esquivel's letter suggests how, time and again, through
her publications, lectures and workshops, as well as through her
unassuming way, Hildegard has been a tower of strength, a friend
and mentor to many.

*****

After Argentina, unrest in Chile after the death of President
Allende and the rise to power of the Pinochet dictatorship prevented Hildegard from going there. Instead, she went to Ecuador
to meet Bishop Leonidas Proaño, himself a mestizo, who identified profoundly with the indigenous peoples and their struggle for
justice. He based evangelization upon respect for the "Indios"
and their way of life, an approach that had lasting impact (from a
personal letter received by Hildegard Goss-Mayr). Hildegard
considered Bishop Proaño an important figure for the wider nonviolent movement. He agreed to come with his co-workers to
Medellin where Jean and Hildegard's allies from across the continent in turn discovered the spiritual power in Proaño's approach.

The Medellin Conference included sixty-five representatives
from twenty-two Latin American countries, the USA, and Europe;
those involved in nonviolent resistance shared their experiences
and developed mutual strategies. Out of this conference emerged
"Servicio Paz y Justicia" ("Service of Peace and Justice," also
known as "Servicio," or "Serpaj"), a people's movement that began to take shape at the Pentecost gathering in Costa Rica. The
conference asked Esquivel to serve as coordinator for Serpaj.
After prayer and reflection, despite the resistance and persecution he expected to face throughout the militarized continent, he
accepted the challenge.

Arrest in Brazil in 1975

Serpaj began during a time of increasing militarization, even as people were beginning to find their voice through grass roots movements for change. Esquivel invited Hildegard, Dr. Mario Carvalho de Jesus, and some workers to hold a seminar in Argentina. Carvalho, a Brazilian, had helped to organize 900 striking workers at "Perus," a cement factory near São Paulo. Despite resistance and repression, the strikers persisted for seven years in Brazil's first explicitly nonviolent campaign. The strike produced a new way of expressing nonviolence: *firmeza permanente*, persistent firmness, similar to Gandhi's "indomitable will." When arrested, Carvalho and other workers, even under torture, treated the jailers, the guards and other prisoners with respect as they presented their cause to them. The workers began to win over journalists, lawyers, and even bishops. After three months, Carvalho was released.

In March of 1975, Hildegard and Mario accepted Adolfo's invitation, but before going to Argentina, they stopped in São Paulo to meet with their ally, Cardinal Arns. While waiting to pick up their luggage at the airport, Hildegard, Mario and Adolfo were arrested by secret police, who placed black hoods over their heads and spirited them away. They responded with prayer and fasting, showing goodwill even to their interrogators and torturers. Cardinal Arns intervened and they were set free, but the experience was nonetheless terrifying. During the mid 1970s, such arrest, imprisonment and torture remained commonplace.

Once, as Hildegard was flying from São Paolo two thousand kilometers north to Recife, she began trembling at the thought that on arrival she could be arrested and no one would know what had happened to her. As she reflected, however, she realized that a circle of courageous colleagues would support her with prayer. Furthermore, she reminded herself, Brazilians lived with this fear all the time. By the time she landed she had an inner calm. That time she was not arrested.

On another occasion when Hildegard and Jean went to Recife, they decided to meet the colonel in charge before trouble could begin. They found that he too wanted reform but considered change agents to be communists. They established a somewhat cordial relationship, and while they were in Recife he left them alone.

When eighty members of the Brazilian chapter of Serpaj, including four bishops as well as Cardinal Arns, convened in São Paulo, the presence of international figures such as Adolfo, Hildegard and Jean provided some degree of protection. They decided to set up Centers for the Protection of Human Rights as a way of shielding and advocating for strikers, for the landless organizing for their rights, and for others the government had targeted. The bishops agreed to take a stand against torture, and in a few months they published a pastoral letter, "Thou Shalt Not Oppress Thy Brothers!" Its unequivocal message helped establish the solidarity of the church with the oppressed and stated clearly its opposition to torture.

Esquivel announced a human rights campaign to culminate on the thirtieth anniversary of the Declaration of Human Rights, December 10, 1978. In the midst of this campaign, on April 4, 1977, the newly established Argentine military junta arrested him in Buenos Aires. While Adolfo was imprisoned, Hildegard and Jean directed a worldwide campaign for his release. They also continued his projects, the most significant being the November 1977 seminar in Bogotá for Latin American bishops on the topic "The Nonviolence of the Bible: Power for Liberation." The church was rediscovering the gospel's witness to and solidarity with the poor, the marginalized, and the forgotten (Goss-Mayr, *Wie Feinde* 64ff).

Cardinal Aloisio Lorscheider, from Fortaleza, Brazil, was particularly important. As president of the Latin American Episcopal Conference (CELAM), he encouraged many bishops to attend the seminar. In his invitation, he spoke of the importance of Hildegard's leadership in "the action of nonviolence" saying "in a world that has forgotten the kindness, sweetness, and gentleness pronounced by Our Lord, she believes that through the constant act of respecting your brother, we can resolve our most difficult problems."

According to Hildegard, two persons were central to the seminar: Padre Alfredinho Kunz and his bishop, Dom Antonio Batista Fragoso of Crateus. Padre Alfredinho, who had been taken prisoner by the Germans in World War II, entered the priesthood late in life. He volunteered to work among the poorest of the poor in northeastern Brazil. In Dom Fragoso's diocese, he found committed poor people whose spirituality drew its power from nonviolent liberation. They stood up for justice without returning evil for evil, certain that good would ultimately triumph (Goss-Mayr, *Wie Feinde* 65ff).

As spiritual leader of the seminar, Padre Alfredinho challenged the participants to commit themselves to liberation of self as well as to the liberation of society. He fasted throughout the conference and called upon everyone to fast together for an entire day. The corporate fast included a time for each person to acknowledge his or her struggle for liberation and to hear the story of one person who had sacrificed as a true Servant of God.

From the time he was appointed bishop in 1964, Dom Fragoso identified with the poor and marginalized. This led the suspicious authorities to place him under surveillance, and to persecute, arrest, and torture priests, nuns and lay people who were following their bishop's example. Fragoso saw his episcopal authority as coming from "the power of love"; as bishop he considered himself not so much the hierarchical head, but the collegial "leader of the power of love."

At first, Dom Fragoso accepted just war as a necessary resort in situations of grave injustice and oppression. But Jean and Hildegard, as did Adolfo Perez Esquivel, encouraged him to follow to its logical conclusion Jesus' way of self-giving love. In time Fragoso and growing numbers of other bishops, priests, nuns and laity rejected violence in the struggle for justice. This nonviolent approach, advocated by Serpaj, came to characterize the path that much of the church took in seeking Latin American liberation.

Hildegard met several times with Archbishop Oscar Romero of San Salvador. He convinced her of the importance of an international campaign of fasting, prayer and political pressure, not only throughout Latin America but also in Europe and in the United States. She traveled to over thirty countries to promote this campaign, convinced of its urgency due to the ominous defamation of Romero and threats on his life.

Mounting violence made the situation seem more and more hopeless. Indeed, the depth of the evil caused Hildegard to become ill. An inflammation in her right arm and hand left her unable to write. Archbishop Romero wrote to her: "I give thanks to you with all my heart for your fraternal solidarity that, from your illness, knows and shares the pain of a people that suffers physically and morally to obtain justice and freedom. And no offering is more effective for the struggle of the Salvadoran people than your suffering united with the liberating pain of Jesus" (from a personal letter received by Hildegard Goss-Mayr). This difficult period convinced her that it is essential to recognize our limits and to rely on God to carry us through.

Archbishop Romero was assassinated as he was saying Mass. His murder made Hildegard realize anew the gospel truth that "the seed must fall to the earth in order to bear fruit." Romero's last sermon (March 23, 1980) witnessed to the truth that prayer and fasting never are in vain:

.... I would like to direct an appeal especially to the members of the Army, and directly to the police and National Guard headquarters, as well as the barracks: you are all brothers of one people, and when you kill farmers, you are killing your brothers. The law of God has precedence over an order to kill which is issued by humans: it says THOU SHALT NOT KILL. No one can be forced to obey an immoral law. It is time to rediscover our own consciences and to place them above an order that commands us to commit a sin. In the name of God and in the name of this suffering people, whose cry rises every day more and more urgently to Heaven, I ask you, I plead with you, I order you: End the oppression!

Earlier that March, contemplating the possibility of his assassination, he said,

I do not believe in death without resurrection. If I am killed, I will rise again in the people of El Salvador. I say this in all humility, without any kind of glorification. As pastor, and according to my calling from God, I am duty-bound to give my life for those I love, and by those I mean all Salvadorans, even those who wish to murder me. If they carry out their threats, I thereby sacrifice my blood, already at this moment, for the healing and resurrection of El Salvador. (Lateinamerika-Rundbrief Nr. 6, IVB, Vienna, June 1980, pp. 1 and 15, quoted in Goss-Mayr, *Wie Feinde* 68)

The price of the liberation struggle was witnessed again and again throughout Latin America, in the martyrdom of religious and lay people, in the imprisonment, torture and disappearance of thousands, and in the continued suffering of the poor. Truly "the blood of the martyrs is the seed of the church." Slowly but surely, small and large, came victories for freedom and justice, love and peace. Yet they came at great cost to those who envisioned a hopeful future, but were willing to pay the price.

The Goss-Mayrs with Archbishop Dom Hélder Câmara
and other Latin American Catholic Leaders

8

"People Power"
in the Philippines

The Goss-Mayrs' work in Latin America did not exclude broadening their worldwide ministry of nonviolence. They were invited to work in Eastern Europe, in the United States and Canada, and in Portugal, Spain, Northern Ireland, Scandinavia and the Balkans, as well as in South Africa, Mozambique, Angola, Rhodesia, Zaire and Tanzania, and the Middle East — in Lebanon and Israel. The nonviolent witness of which Hildegard and Jean were such a vital part was growing around the world, and they responded to invitations in country after country.

Perhaps the most dramatic nonviolent struggle was in the Philippines, once a colony of Spain, then, after the Spanish-American war, of the United States. The island nation became independent after World War II and established a democratic government modeled after America's.

By the mid 1980s, under President Ferdinand Marcos, the Philippines had moved from democratic rule to dictatorship. The people responded to worsening socioeconomic conditions and growing human rights violations with protest rallies and strikes. A revolutionary Maoist group, the New Peoples' Army (NPA), mounted an armed response. Instead of seeing the protests and armed struggle as symptoms of the need for constructive change, Marcos claimed that the unrest was the problem, a situation which he claimed the communists were exploiting. Encouraged by the

United States, which saw him as a reliable anti-communist ally, Marcos declared martial law and took harsh action against his challengers.

He imprisoned his most popular political opponent, Senator Benigno Aquino. During eight years of solitary confinement, Aquino grew in devotion to prayer. Studying the Bible and the writings of Gandhi convinced him of the truth and efficacy of following God through liberating nonviolence. He grew more and more convinced of the need for a revolutionary but nonviolent challenge to the Marcos government. Senator Aquino was allowed to go to the United States to obtain medical treatment for a dangerous heart condition. On his return, however, as he got off the plane at Manila International Airport on August 21, 1983, he was assassinated. Aquino's death fueled opposition to Marcos, who many believed had ordered the assassination.

Yet there was no consensus about the *means* to be used in opposing President Marcos. Many, including a number of dedicated Christians, supported the NPA because they saw violence as the only effective response to someone like Marcos. He was called "a Hitler of Southeast Asia," who would stop at nothing to maintain power. Others, however, were drawn to the nonviolent Gandhian and Christian advocacy of their fallen leader, Senator Aquino. Among those sympathizers were the Little Sisters of Jesus, a community of nuns working in a Manila barrio. Like their founder, Charles de Foucauld, they led a life of contemplation and service to the poorest of the poor.

They knew what Jean and Hildegard had done in Eastern Europe and Latin America, and so invited them to the Philippines to observe and assess the situation, and to help however they could. Jean and Hildegard, after prayerful reflection, decided to accept the invitation and arrived in February 1984. They traveled around the country studying the social conditions and meeting members of the anti-Marcos opposition. They witnessed the poverty of the barrios, and of the farmers, sugar cane workers, and factory workers. They met with opposition intellectuals, labor leaders and academics. They found that many church leaders had aligned themselves with the rich and the powerful. Nonetheless, they met an impressive number of bishops, nuns, priests, and seminarians who were working for non-violent change. This number included charismatic leaders like the Bishop Francisco Claver, who had organized nonviolent resistance to government injustice against the indigenous people of northern Luzon and who later had led in the formation of Christian base communities in his diocese on the large southern island of Mindanao. His courageous pastoral letters helped build resistance among the laity.

Hildegard and Jean met Corazon Aquino, widow of the slain senator, as well as other members of his family. This talented, prominent family's commitment impressed them. Corazon considered herself apolitical, but had great leadership skills. Aquino's youngest brother, Agapito (nicknamed "Butz"), had founded an action group named "ATOM" (acronym for "August 21 Movement"). He told Jean and Hildegard that leftists had offered him weapons if he would join the armed struggle against the Marcos government. The plea of Butz and others for help in building the strong, deep nonviolent movement that Senator Aquino had envisioned convinced the Goss-Mayrs that they should help.

They needed to return to Europe but promised to come back if prayerful reflection confirmed the decision. The Marcos government was powerful. Its challengers were many but divided. Could the nonviolent adherents endure a long, difficult struggle? Would the church support the Aquino forces or maintain its relationship with those who held military, economic, and governmental power?

In the midst of these considerations they received word that ATOM, encouraged and guided by Father Jose Blanco, a Jesuit, had fasted for ten days for purification and discernment in the task that lay ahead of them. At the end of the fast their commitment was clear, and they contacted Jean and Hildegard. This call convinced the Goss-Mayrs that indeed they should return, which they did in June 1984.

With the leadership of Fr. Blanco, they quietly arranged a network of places (such as houses of religious orders in out-of-the-way locations) to hold seminars around the country, and invited trustworthy persons who had shown a commitment, or at least a strong interest in, the challenge of radical nonviolence. They had to be careful lest informers and spies disrupt the seminars. They invited a diverse group, including nuns, priests and laypeople, academics, students, political leaders, labor leaders and workers, for the most part Catholic but also including some Protestants, Muslims, and people of goodwill with no particular religious affiliation. As the Gandhian movement did in India, they cast a wide and inclusive net. The U.S. Fellowship of Reconciliation and Union Theological Seminary of the Philippines conducted a parallel effort (in which I took part) to facilitate non-violence workshops with ministers, church workers and laity in Protestant institutions and with networks of other people sympathetic to the cause.

Jean and Hildegard developed a compelling way of presenting the core beliefs of Christian nonviolence, rooted in the Gospel but also shaped by Gandhian methodology. As they presented material, they divided the participants into small groups to explore their questions and share their own insights and experiences. They allotted time for developing campaign strategies and tactics. Over their days together, group solidarity and resolve grew, strengthened by worship and time set aside for personal meditation as well.

The rigorous seminars introduced the participants to active non-violence, including its religious and humanistic roots, as well as the history of its testing and methods in South Africa and India, in the American civil rights movement, and in Latin American liberation struggles. Analyzing the national situation revealed how the establishment rested upon certain pillars of support — the army, corporations, the media, passive and fearful workers, the middle class, intellectuals, and silent churches. Toppling or even weakening these pillars could change the status quo.

Many found a stumbling block in the seminars' teaching that everyone, including enemies, deserves absolute respect. They found it almost equally difficult to accept that violence operates not just in opponents, but in everyone. The potential for evil resides not just in "the other," but in every human heart. Patient and convincing teaching, reinforced with time for prayer and reflection, could root out the violence in oneself, and reveal how to find the image of God even in those who did evil deeds.

Jean and Hildegard's experience with similar situations in Latin America, as well as with Nazis during World War II and Communists during the Cold War, validated the transformative, revolutionary power of active nonviolence. Hildegard spoke strongly and clearly: "The seed of the violence is in the structures, of course, and in the dictator. But isn't it also in ourselves? It's very easy to say that Marcos is the evil. But unless we each tear the dictator out of our own heart, nothing will change. Another group will come into power and will act similarly to those whom they replaced" (Goss-Mayr, "When Prayer and Revolution," pp. 116ff in this publication).

The seminar participants tested themselves. Although all shared a common opposition to Marcos, they also bore other antagonisms such as between landlords and farmers, or between politicians and their distrustful constituents. Gifted individuals such as Father Jose Blanco and Tess Ramiro helped to Filipinize the deliberations, that is, to convey the seminars' content not as Austrians or Frenchmen or Brazilians would, but through the culture and outlook of Asians. From the outset Jean and Hildegard noted the Filipino gift of drawing upon their own cultural traditions and experiences. For example, distrust and antipathy between participants could lead to shaming or loss of face and in turn could disrupt the training. Fr. Blanco celebrated the Eucharist using large wafers so that two people who mistrusted or disliked each other could break the bread and seek forgiveness together. This led to other ways of learning to deal with opponents, even enemy soldiers, in unexpected, healing ways. For example, seeing soldiers not as uniformed brutes but as conscripted peasants (the way Jean had learned to think of Nazi soldiers when he was a prisoner of war) allowed unexpected responses to emerge. Hence, the participants were learning not just a methodology of social change but a spiritual grounding upon which to carry it out.

On one occasion Butz Aquino was called out of a seminar to help defuse a crisis during a march on Malacañang, the presidential palace. The army had faced off with anti-Marcos forces on the Mendiola Bridge leading to the palace, which was off limits to demonstrators.

This situation provided a test case for developing a Filipino strategy to avoid rioting and killing. Armed troops faced the approaching demonstrators, at the front of whom were seminarians. If the crowd were to move too far the soldiers would have fired, as they had been trained to do. Butz persuaded the crowd to allow the seminarians in their distinctive white cassocks to slowly, deliberately move to the middle of the bridge, stopping near the soldiers. He presumed that the soldiers, most of them also Catholic, would hesitate to attack them. Then, as Butz approached the general in charge and offered his hand in friendship, the seminarians began reciting aloud the Lord's Prayer in Tagalog. All of the demonstrators joined in, then even the soldiers. The showdown ended peacefully.

What came to be called the "People Power Revolution" was beginning. Bishop Claver took the necessary step of trying to win the support of the Roman Catholic hierarchy, most of whom had supported Marcos. Claver invited all 110 bishops to a seminar, fifteen of whom were able to attend. In their sessions with the Goss-Mayrs, they struggled with their own complicity in the violence of the dictatorship. Like their counterparts in the 1977 meeting of bishops in Bogotá, they experienced the radical call to follow Jesus nonviolently, standing with the poor and the oppressed. With this experience, the fifteen then went to the annual meeting of the Filipino bishops to bear witness about active nonviolence and to call on them to join the people in the emerging struggle. The assembled bishops, deeply moved, issued a pastoral letter condemning the dictatorship (Goss-Mayr, *Wie Feinde* 74).

After all of the seminars with the many different groups had ended, the participants met to share their experiences and reflect on the future. At this meeting, July 10, 1984, AKKAPKA was founded. AKKAPKA is the acronym for the Tagalog title "Aksyon Para sa Kapayapaan at Katarungan," "Action for Peace and Justice." The acronym was chosen to express the Tagalog phrase "akap ka" which can be translated "I embrace you." Under the leadership of Fr. Blanco and Tess Ramiro, AKKAPKA held forty seminars in the following year in thirty provinces, helping spread a nonviolent movement that was faithful to the vision and hope of the martyred Senator "Ninoy" Aquino. At this hour of crisis the nonviolent teachings of Jesus and Gandhi, himself an Asian, were taking root in Filipino soil. AKKAPKA members published a pamphlet that contained this Credo:

> We are a people of God.
> We believe in justice, democracy and peace.
> But most of all in the absolute value of the human being.
>
> We are opposed to all forms of injustice and oppression
>   now prevalent in our society.
> Any authoritarian form of government,
> The discrimination against the poor
> The gross violation of human rights
> The foreign domination over our economic, political
>   and cultural system.
> We espouse a society that fosters
> Equality,
> Protects the rights
> And holds sacred the dignity of every person.
>
> We commit ourselves to the construction
> And preservation of a just Filipino society.
>
> But in all our deeds, we vow:
> Never to kill
> Never to hurt
> To convert our oppressors to the truth
>   and to remain united in our struggle.
>
> And that this Credo may become
> A way of life,
> We humbly call on God
> To favor us with his help.
> We ask each sister and brother
> To tell us when we fail to be true to this Credo.

Late in 1985 Marcos surprised everyone by calling for a "snap" election to demonstrate that he was not a dictator, but that he had the

people's support. The opposition, however, began to coalesce behind Corazon "Cory" Aquino, whose image of courage, compassion
and incorruptibility gave the determined Filipino people hope. Her
slain husband's call for a nonviolent revolution had been reinforced
in the Goss-Mayrs' nonviolence seminars that she had attended.

Cory Aquino did not seek to be a presidential candidate, but after
prayerful reflection and seeing widespread support, she decided to
run. Despite Marcos' power and wealth, as well as his control of the
media and of the armed forces, the desire for change and the popularity of Corazon Aquino swept the country. Her supporters employed
what they called "people power," which included innovative nonviolent tactics. In "prayer tents" her supporters gathered not only to
pray, but also to fast, reflect, and plan. Precinct by precinct people
were trained to guard the polls and to ensure the votes were fairly
counted. When Marcos agents sought to "fix" the election, the com-
puter operators tabulating the ballots risked their lives by calling a
press conference to report that the results being published differed
from the landslide for Aquino that they were counting.

Fearful of martial law, Aquino called together hundreds of her
best workers for a day of strategizing. Jean and Hildegard were invited to take part in these critical discussions. Out of the meeting
came a plan for protracted civil disobedience that could last for
months and spread throughout the archipelago. After the strategy
session, the Goss-Mayrs returned to Europe. At that moment no one
foresaw what would unfold in the coming days.

The Minister of Defense and the head of the armed forces, with a
small contingent of 250 men, left the Marcos government and declared their allegiance to Aquino, whom they said was the legitimate
winner of the election. Marcos' swift reaction to this mutiny was met
by hundreds of thousands of Aquino supporters, who surrounded the
defectors in a creative, yet dangerous display of nonviolent power.

Cardinal Jaime Sin, Archbishop of Manila, was well acquainted
with Hildegard and Jean from his many discussions with them about
the gospel and nonviolence. He and Butz Aquino gave a national radio address urgently calling on the people to support the defectors.
The call was unambiguously nonviolent: everyone was to leave all

weapons at home. The people were to form a protective wall around the defectors that would prevent the army from entering their camp. The Cardinal specifically requested of the contemplative orders of nuns: "The country is on the verge of civil war. Pray and fast to prevent this from happening."

Hundreds, then thousands, then hundreds of thousands began coming to the camp of the defectors, who expected that at any moment soldiers loyal to President Marcos would attack. The people were determined but nonviolent. Astonishingly, they met Marcos' soldiers with gifts of sandwiches, flowers, and goodwill. Masses of people in the roads prayed and sang as they blocked the soldiers and their vehicles. Some, including Butz Aquino, sat in front of tanks, while others climbed up on armored personnel carriers to plead with the soldiers.

Through the transistor radios that many carried, the Catholic Radio Veritas and its nationwide network of stations broadcast continually. The broadcasters knew about nonviolent struggle. They read from the writings of Benigno Aquino, Gandhi and King, as well as the Sermon on the Mount. They provided their listeners — "the unarmed forces of the Philippines" — with the latest information on what was happening, such as troop movements and places needing reinforcement. Stories from seminar trainings — such as that of the Czech students in 1968 sitting down in front of Russian tanks, and of Gandhi's followers on the march offering no violent response when they were beaten — permeated the ranks of this new kind of army. To Marcos' soldiers, Radio Veritas said, "Refuse unjust orders. You are called to serve the Filipino people, not just one man." Broadcasts by Cardinal Sin, Butz Aquino, and Cory Aquino informed the nation of the rapidly unfolding events (Goss-Mayr, *Wie Feinde* 72-79).[1] When Marcos' forces destroyed its transmitter, Radio Veritas switched to a back-up. The international press, radio, and television shared these dramatic events with the world.

---

1. A complete account of these events is found in Jim and Nancy Forest's, *Four Days in February. The Story of the Nonviolent Overthrow of the Marcos Regime* (Basingstoke, UK: Marshall Pickering, 1988). See also the special issue on Philippine People Power in the March 1987 issue of *Fellowship* Magazine.

In only a few days the once mighty Marcos collapsed and he, his wife and their entourage were allowed to flee the country. Corazon Aquino was the stunning victor in an election that, like the Gandhian struggle for India's freedom and the U.S. civil rights movement, displayed to the whole world the ability of a people, armed only with truth, nonviolence and determination, to change the course of history. Indeed, in the second half of the twentieth century the image of the armed revolutionary began to give way to that of unarmed freedom fighter — not physically strong, armed guerillas but unarmed men, women and young people, even the elderly and children, massing on the streets, sitting in front of tanks, reaching out in friendship to armed soldiers. Sister Marlene-Karla, of the Little Sisters of Jesus, said that Jean and Hildegard were the midwives for the birth of nonviolence in the Philippines. Cardinal Sin said that their seminars in nonviolent resistance trained people for this "revolution of love" (Franklin).

In one sense, the long-term impact of "people power" has been disappointing. As Hildegard points out, the revolution came too quickly. Based in Manila and Quezon City, it had only a limited reach into the provinces. Politically it was important to remove the dictator and to allow important democratic changes such as free elections, a new constitution, and a trustworthy government free of authoritarian rule. But entrenched economic institutions and lack of support from the middle and upper classes prevented "people power" from planting deep roots. The giant step of toppling the dictator was only a beginning in what Gandhi called "experimenting with Truth." We need to learn far more about the understanding and practical application of nonviolence.[2] Nonetheless, active nonviolence has enormous potential; its relevance and power has been demonstrated as it has spread globally. In the years following 1986, further events built upon this dynamic legacy of *satyagraha,* "Truth Force," as revealed in the largely nonviolent collapse of the Soviet bloc, the triumph over apartheid in South Africa, and the peaceful ending of many dictatorships in Latin America.

---

2. See Jonathan Schell's seminal *The Unconquerable World. Power, Nonviolence, and the Will of the People* (New York: Henry Holt and Company, 2003).

9

Forces Vives in Africa

Eastern Europe. The Soviet Union. Latin America. Asia. With indefatigable energy, Hildegard and Jean took the message of nonviolent liberation around the world. Word spread to peoples' movements, other groups and individuals about their expertise. Historically astute, culturally sensitive, hard working and modest, they gained a reputation as being informed, winsome teachers and facilitators of transformative nonviolence.

Africa, a continent subjected for centuries to colonial conquest and rule, also became an arena for their work. European powers seeking to exploit Africa's rich natural resources (such as gold, diamonds, oil, cobalt and phosphates) and its geopolitically strategic locations had established colonies, in the process dividing its more than 2,000 ethnic groups, with distinct languages and histories, into artificial political entities. Transportation and communication were developed, but primarily to meet colonial purposes. At the end of World War II, all of the Third World, including Africa, sought freedom, their high expectations expressed in a variety of liberation struggles and movements. Jean and Hildegard, with their growing expertise and reputation, found many opportunities to teach nonviolence in Africa.

In 1973 during a visit to Portugal, their witness for nonviolence led friends there to share with them the repressive situation in that country's African colonies, Angola and Mozambique. No government had resisted challenges to colonial rule more fiercely than did the Salazar dictatorship in Portugal. Nonetheless the peoples' awakening and unstoppable demand for freedom grew, part of an irreversible tide sweeping the world.

As in other places, the Goss-Mayrs' invitations sometimes came from an individual or group that defended human rights, resisted oppression or simply tried to live according to the way of Jesus. Mostly, however, they were invited by some segment of the church — a bishop or lay group, a catechetical center, a community of nuns or a social action committee. Such invitations revealed the complexity of the problem, as these groups often differed with or even were opposed by elements in the church, reinforced by racism and patriarchy, that tolerated or even supported colonial governments and their policies.

From 1973 through the 1980s, Jean and Hildegard returned again and again to Africa. They worked in Mozambique and Angola, in South Africa, Tanzania and Southern Rhodesia (Zimbabwe), Congo (which became Zaire and now once again is called Democratic Republic of the Congo) and Madagascar, particularly with nonviolent groups dealing with human rights issues, ethnic conflicts and reconciliation. In April 1991, while preparing to return to Madagascar, Jean Goss unexpectedly died. We will return to this later, but for now we will trace the continuation of the work in Africa after Jean's death. Despite urgent invitations from other parts of the world, Hildegard continued this important ministry, concentrating her energies as much as possible in Africa.

In the 1990s and into the new millennium, Hildegard worked in Madagascar, the Ivory Coast, Congo-Brazzaville, Rwanda, Zaire, Chad, Burundi and Kenya. Often she worked with teacher/trainers from various Fellowship of Reconciliation branches in Belgium, Switzerland, and especially France; sometimes she went alone. Over the years her work was supported by the prayers of communities of nuns, especially the contemplative orders.

The projects placed heavy demands on her. These extensive travels to countries often in turmoil and with extreme climates demanded rigorous physical and spiritual strength. Each location required intensive preparation, and careful listening and communication skills during the seminars. The long journeys to places beset by tropical heat and diseases could have discouraged even a young person, much less ones in their seventies. Through constant vigilance to obtain necessary inoculations and potable water, Jean and Hildegard were blessed never to have contracted malaria or other tropical diseases.

Usually the children stayed in Europe to maintain their schooling and to take advantage of a stable home, friends and family. Long days of shipboard travel provided time for relaxation, reading and contemplation. In time air travel made their travels more efficient, but also allowed much less time for transition from one country to the next. Jean and Hildegard sought to keep their lives in balance through study, prayer and meditation, as well as healthful exercise such as walking and swimming. Their love of music led them to attend concerts and cultural events whenever possible. They read a lot, sometimes to each other.

Like her patron saint and namesake, Hildegard of Bingen, Hildegard loves solitude and the contemplation of nature. She enjoys holding a chestnut in her hand, saying that round things convey our world and our oneness in it. She has found inspiration in this great woman medieval mystic, whose spirituality embraces the whole universe, a universe infused by a living light. Hildegard of Bingen's unique mixture of activism and mysticism generated a prophetic concern for all of life. Her concern for justice also led her at times to confront ecclesiastical and governmental authorities.

The physical challenges the Goss-Mayrs faced in Africa paralleled the great changes taking place there. Colonialism was giving way to independence but the new regimes that drew support from the former colonial powers often wound up suppressing the dreams of freedom, and often allowed themselves to be drawn into the Cold War rivalry between capitalist and communist worlds.

Amid these vast changes, some maintained their commitment to fostering democratic values and practices that drew upon the Gospel as well as recovering nonviolent indigenous practices and beliefs that respected human rights, cooperative efforts and inclusive community. Jean and Hildegard's seminars emphasized recovering indigenous traditions that colonial policies and points of view had

often disregarded. Hildegard refers to these ancient beliefs and practices as pillars of nonviolence. This openness to and respect for
people's traditions and practices provided part of the basis for a new
vision for a changed era.

Hildegard gives an example of discovering ways to build a new syn-
thesis from the past. The *palaver* is an African tradition in which a whole
community, aided by a mediator, enables everyone to be heard before a
decision is made. It includes a number of nonviolent rules, such as

- taking time in resolving a conflict, waiting at least for another day;
- assigning a person of wisdom and moral authority as mediator;
- scheduling the *palaver* early in the day so everyone can
  participate;
- signifying that a quarrel is settled by pouring water over
  the earth, a sign of reconciliation that washes away bitter-
  ness and revenge;
- including restitution in the settlement of a quarrel;
- valuing children (especially important in conflicts over
  polygamy)
- reintegrating persons into the community by depicting
  their suffering through rituals;
- dealing with bad news carefully so as not to hurt unduly the
  person concerned;
- providing opportunities for forgiveness and reconciliation
  through marriages between members of different ethnic
  groups;
- extending hospitality towards everyone;
- wherever necessary, giving help in solidarity.
  (Goss-Mayr, *Wie Feinde* 89ff)

These traditional values harmonize with the gospel values
of absolute respect for the human person, care for the earth, hon-
oring human rights, resolving conflict nonviolently and building
an inclusive community. Together they form a center of renewal
and resistance against both dictatorial state power and neoliberal
capitalism.

Their work in Portugal provided the initial incentive for the Goss-Mayrs to visit Africa that would continue for decades into many countries and varied situations. In Mozambique and Angola, scarred by the dictatorship that dominated both home and colony, Marxist resistance had sprung up in the guerilla movement Frelimo. While many local institutions supported and were protected by Portuguese rule, some voices — white and black — longed for a message like the one Jean and Hildegard brought and wanted to work for peace and justice.

During their first visit to Mozambique, despite surveillance by the secret police (PIDE), the Goss-Mayrs found support from Bishop Manuel Vieira Pinto in Nampula and from Catechetical Centers that had been established by the Peres Blancs (the White Fathers). Courageous laity in the capital, Lourenço Marques, also helped to build a network for nonviolent action. Similarly, Angolan bishops, priests and lay people were open and eager for training in nonviolence. The situation, however, was not favorable for the long-term building of nonviolent groups there, even though Jean worked hard among blacks as well as whites. Follow-up work continued a year later. Despite initial success, however, a long civil war fed by the East/West conflict forced all those committed to nonviolent action out of the country.

Because of her fluency in English, Hildegard was able to spread the message of nonviolence in South Africa, sharing news of the nonviolent movement in other parts of the world and explaining the difficulties as well as the long-range benefits of such struggle. Around the country Catholic bishops as well as the Commission for Justice and Reconciliation of the Protestant South Africa Council of Churches, showed great interest. She also met with Quakers, Mennonites, and their networks.

Both black and white South Africans expressed keen interest, some saying they had never before heard this message of gospel-based nonviolence. The event that seemed to excite Hildegard the most was her meeting black Christian women in Soweto, who spoke of the Bible as the source of revolutionary, transformative Love. She discussed conscientious objection and civil disobedience with white Christians working in solidarity with those seeking an end to apartheid (Goss-Mayr, *Wie Feinde* 90).

After 1983 the government refused Hildegard a visa so she was restricted to visiting Lesotho, the small black republic within South Africa. It proved important as the Transformation Resource Center came to be located in its capital, Maseru. She also received help from South African FOR members such as the Presbyterian minister Rob Robertson and his wife, Gertrude, but by that time FOR was banned from operating as an organization.

English members of the FOR in Rhodesia (Zimbabwe) invited Hildegard during the extraordinary situation in 1965 when Ian Smith declared Rhodesia an independent nation. Groups responded violently as well as nonviolently. Hildegard met with committed persons suffering for their radical nonviolent commitment and work. These meetings planted seeds that years later grew into a Zimbabwe FOR branch.

Zaire

In 1986 and again in 1989, during the repressive Mobutu dictatorship, the Goss-Mayrs were invited to a number of Catholic dioceses in Zaire. Despite the fear and suspicion that their harsh experience under Mobutu had generated in the people, Jean's experience as a veteran of war and imprisonment gave him the sensitivity to get through to them. Even though he spoke French, as did the people of Zaire, Jean still had to overcome the obstacles of his own race and nationality, which represented Western colonialism. With refreshing candor, he did not deny his heritage but contrasted his own national origins with the liberating power of the gospel that casts out fear and opens the way of justice, peace, truth and freedom. Similarly, Hildegard acknowledged her European origins, but turned the focus of her remarks to the universal gospel that transcends nation and race.

Jean's seminars gave rise to a number of cells of nonviolent resistance and hope, such as the group "Amos" in Kinshasa and Mbuji-mayi. On February 16, 1992, following church services, the charismatic Abbe Jose Mpundu led a March for Hope that included nearly a million people, singing, praying the rosary, and carrying statues. Mobutu's security forces shot at them, killing at least thirty and wounding hundreds.

The march generated base communities throughout the country, determined to build a new society. Abbe Mpundu observed, "The people, who have overcome their fear, have finally understood that they must liberate themselves or never be free. They have risen and will retreat no more.... Through the march the people have shown that democracy does not mean conquest of power for the sake of power, but with the aim of a new way of life" (Goss-Mayr, *Wie Feinde* 90).

Rwanda

Hildegard returned again and again to Africa — to the Ivory Coast, Congo-Brazzaville, Rwanda, Eastern Zaire and Chad. In 1993, invited by the Congregation of the White Fathers, she went to Rwanda and the nearby towns of Goma and Bukavu in Zaire. The breathtaking beauty of the region belied the ominous development of hostility between Hutus and Tutsis, fed by poverty and a burgeoning population. Conflict and murder spread throughout the country. Unlike Radio Veritas in the Philippines, the vicious and racist "Radio of the Thousand Hills" inflamed peoples' fear and hatred, strengthening extremist groups.

Hildegard's seminars generated a peace march for January 1, 1994, at a hopeful time when the treaty of Arusha was being negotiated. By the thousands, representing a spectrum of Christian churches and encouraged by the Vatican and the World Council of Churches, Tutsis and Hutus from across the country marched together in Kigali and other towns. The people's hopes poured out on the streets as they embraced, weeping and praying. At the end of the march Hildegard said, "Like the Christians of the early Church, we stand before the Cross, facing agony. But the Spirit of the living God will not abandon us and will lead us to resurrection" (Goss-Mayr, *Wie Feinde* 91).

Despite this spark of hope, the forces of darkness continued to grow. Only a few months later, on their way home from Arusha,

Rwandan President Juvenal Habyarimana's personal plane was shot down killing him, Burundian president Cyprien Ntarymira, and members of their entourages. The genocide that ensued left hundreds of thousands dead and created two million refugees.

In the face of such bloodletting, Hildegard reminds us that such evil cannot snuff out the power of God's love. Known only to a few, many acts of kindness and courage occurred, as shown in these words of Georgette Leonard, sister of the Missionaries of Our Beloved Lady of Africa, who writes of her experience with the people in Busogo during the massacre on April 7, 1994:

> When the militias, furnished with lists of names, cowardly murdered families that had sought protection with us, when the [militias] threatened to kill us too, you were there, interposed yourself again and again and negotiated with a bravery which we did not know in you.
>
> Thank you neighbors, for staying with us during the long hours when the militia interrogated us. How faithful you were to our friendship, which was thus confirmed in the most difficult of times. By receiving us, you saved us!
>
> Thank you my friends for coming to us on the morning after our escape. Never will I forget your long, silent handclasp, your sad eyes which expressed your affection and your pity. Thank you too, dear, old grandmother, who had been fleeing already for such a long time. You embraced me and said: "Patience, you will go back, you will rebuild!"
>
> Thank you, my sister, my brother from Rwanda: you opened your doors last year already, accepted five, ten, twenty and more refugees to stay with you, and shared everything, your roof, harvest and your last supplies. How many still share today according to old tradition.
>
> Thank you too, refugees. I admire the courage you have to smile, yes, sometimes even to dance with the children in front of your tents made of branches and canvas!
>
> What vital strength! Stronger than death! For me, dear friends, you are witnesses of "humanity" and hope for the Rwanda of tomorrow! (Goss-Mayr, *Wie Feinde* 92)

Such unheralded charity planted the seeds of new life, such as in the case of the Center for Reconciliation in Butare whose presence in the 1993 nonviolence seminars witnessed strongly to the work of justice, reconciliation and forgiveness. A Hutu, lay theologian Laurien Ntezimana, and a Tutsi, Abbe Modeste Mungwarareba, had established "cells of peace" at the University of Butare and in villages nearby. They survived the genocide but their center was destroyed and staff members murdered.

The Center has gradually resumed its work. In a country traumatized by genocide, the message of active nonviolence has never seemed more difficult or more essential.

Chad

The situation Hildegard found in Chad reflected the tensions between the faithful of different religions found in many other parts of the world. In the north, in the Sahel desert, live Arabic-speaking Muslim cattle breeders. In the south, large numbers of animist farmers had converted to Christianity. Muslim fundamentalists from nearby Sudan provoked tension and violence between the two groups. Nonetheless, Chadians strove to build a democratic civil society that would transcend tribal and religious differences. "Chad Nonviolence," a vibrant youth movement formed in 1991, is an example of a group committed to finding peaceful solutions to national, tribal and religious problems.

Hildegard facilitated seminars between Christians and Muslims who sought nonviolent dimensions within their respective faiths. She shared insights from the predominantly Muslim FOR branch in Bangladesh, which includes Hindu and Christian members. The seminars took their daily meditations from the Koran, the Bible and the writings of Mohandas Gandhi, Martin Luther King, Jr., and Rabindanath Tagore. This approach resembled Gandhi's interfaith practice while walking through Indian villages, even during times of hostility or violence.

The manifesto of the 1994 peace march in Kigali expresses the potential of these nonviolent efforts:

Human life is holy and inviolable.

No to violence: no to the destruction of our land.

No to lies, hypocrisy and manipulation.

We want peace and pledge ourselves to be instruments of this peace.

We want life from the power of love and nonviolence.

We demand that truth, justice, and tolerance become the basis of our society.

We pledge ourselves:

> to take responsibility upon ourselves,
> to bring violence to a halt through peaceful means,
> to work for political and economic justice,
> to plant the seeds for a democratic culture,
> to help humane and Christian values to unfold.

The only path for us is the democratic path, for a democracy which engages the whole people, a democracy which we build together in tolerance and dialogue with respect for human rights. (Goss-Mayr, *Wie Feinde* 94ff)

Madagascar

The extraordinary events during historic changes in Madagascar included Jean and Hildegard's unusual yet significant contribution.

Following the 1986 People Power Revolution in the Philippines, the Goss-Mayrs were invited to Madagascar. Other commitments prevented them, so they sent tapes, videos and printed materials to various ecumenical groups working for an end to the Didier Ratsiraka dictatorship.

Protestant English missionaries introduced Christianity to Madagascar in the early nineteenth century, followed fifty years later by French Catholics. In time the churches assumed a significant role in the affairs of the island. In 1896 France assumed colonial administration. After World War II a movement for independence asserted itself in Madagascar, as it had in many other parts of the world. At

first this movement was nonviolent, but an unexpected armed re-
bellion in 1947 led to French repression that did not ease until 1958,
when independence was granted. The military, however, soon
seized power, designating Ratsiraka dictator. Through the 1980s
he implemented North Korean style socialism, a totalitarian model
that threatened to destroy the nation; by 1990 Madagascar had become the sixteenth poorest country in the world (Goss-Mayr, *Wie
Feinde* 82ff).

A ray of hope in this bleak period was the ecumenical commitment of Protestants and Catholics through the Christian Council of
Churches and the *Forces Vives*. In Madagascar, as in Ivory Coast,
Zaire, Congo and Benin, autonomous national conferences developed, uniting all the active forces of society — *Forces Vives,* as they
were called — to replace tribal conflict with democratically inspired
national unity. In 1985, to mark the 150th anniversary of the translation of the Bible into Madagascan, they celebrated the human rights
and freedom found in the Bible. Madagascar's Council of Churches
held two national congresses that built upon the global changes that
followed the 1986 People Power Revolution in the Philippines. In
the second congress the potential of *Forces Vives* revealed itself, under the leadership of a surgeon, Albert Zafy.

Also during 1986 Paul-Alfonse Ravoavy, a Benedictine monk
from Madagascar, happened to attend a lecture by Jean and Hildegard
at La Pierre-qui-Vire, a Benedictine Abbey near Dijon, France, in
which they explained how Philippine People Power had nonviolently
overthrown the Marcos dictatorship. During a conversation with the
Goss-Mayrs afterwards, Fr. Ravoavy raised the possibility that such
a change could come to his country. He returned to Madagascar with books, tapes, and videos that documented and illustrated
the possibilities (Goss-Mayr, *Wie Feinde* 81). In the name of the
Catholic Bishops' Conference of Madagascar, Bishop Jean-Marie
Rakotondrasoa, president of its Commission on Justice and Peace,
invited the Goss-Mayrs to help develop their nascent efforts to
strengthen the nonviolent commitment in the churches.

In March of 1991 Hildegard went to Vienna to attend to her
mother, who was very ill. When Hildegard returned to Paris on

Wednesday of Holy Week, Jean surprised her with a bouquet of freesias, their favorite flower, saying, "It should be like our wedding
day!" Hildegard reflects on that joyous moment: "Easter, the feast of
resurrection, filled both of us with joy and new hope: yes, Jesus, who
had overcome sin and death, is alive in our world. Hate and violence
will not have the last word." They prepared to depart for Madagascar
just after Easter, on April 4. But at dawn on April 3, Jean died. They
had been wed on Easter and now, during Easter week, his life ended.
In his final weeks Jean had contended with apocalyptic nightmares
and an aging, weakened body. Nonetheless, he never ceased attending peace rallies. This grand old man of nonviolence went resolutely
with his cane, encouraging the youth to hold fast to their witness
against war and to embody the vision of transformative nonviolence.
He sensed that his life was nearing its end. He wrote his friends that
he would soon be in God's embrace, saying, "You cannot imagine
how wonderful it will be. I pray that I may give witness up until my
last breath: taken from my work right into heaven." He had a
mystical belief that, freed of his bodily limitations, he would continue his work beyond the grave, alongside his beloved Hildegard
(Goss-Mayr, *Wie Feinde* 80).

The funeral Mass at the Saint Jacques du Haut Pas Church in
Paris overflowed with people who sang, "Il est vraiment ressuscite,
ne cherchez pas parmi les morts!" (He is truly risen, why do you
seek him among the dead!) On his plain wooden coffin lay a bouquet of freesias (Goss-Mayr, *Wie Feinde* 81).

Not ignoring her personal grief and loss, Hildegard sees Jean's
death in the context of the momentous changes taking place in the
world. The end of the Cold War had raised hopes that long-deferred
human needs would be met now that the raison d'être of the worldwide arms race had ended. Instead, the construction of weapons
and research for new, even deadlier ways of killing continued. The
continuing strife in the Middle East, especially in Iraq, tempted
Hildegard to despair that the opportunities for a peaceful world
were slipping away. The mindset of lethal conflict is hard to dis-
lodge, even in the face of the new, more humane and hopeful
changes.

With faith in the resurrection, those in the nonviolent movement of Madagascar who were planning Jean's visit believed that
he would be with them as they themselves carried out his program.
The culmination came on April 21 when 400 gathered at the College Saint-Antoine in Antananarivo. A video of Jean's life was
shown and the celebration of the Eucharist was the climax of the
program. Reflecting on this, Hildegard observed:

> It is not part of our rational European way of thinking to
> fathom the mystical and mythical depth of foreign cultures
> like the direct, intimate tie connecting the living and the
> dead in Madagascar. When I visited Madagascar in the late
> fall of 1991 and again in 1992, Jean with his prophetic, rous-
> ing, burning power of love and truth was so palpably
> present, that I no longer hesitated to say: "Yes, Jean was a
> prophetic instrument for the founding of organized, active
> nonviolence in Madagascar which has substantially influ-
> enced the *Forces Vives* in their fight against the exploitative
> Ratsiraka regime." (Goss-Mayr, *Wie Feinde* 81)

On the night of April 21, a strong tremor shook Antananarivo. It
caused little damage but the participants took it as a sign that Jean
was urging them to move forward boldly. A week later, on May 1, the
Forces Vives publicly challenged the Ratsiraka dictatorship. Widespread nonviolent demonstrations took place, with strikes in the
schools, railways, banks, postal services and governmental offices.
For six months the nation was brought to a standstill. High ranking
military and police figures sided with the demonstrators. Twice a
week 100,000 to 200,000 gathered for strikes and demonstrations.

Albert Zafy established an opposition unity government, with
headquarters in a Protestant-run college. He asked the Council of
Churches to serve a mediating role. Hildegard sent a letter to the
Catholic bishops' conference, which had gathered in an emer-
gency session. Referring to the key role Filipino bishops had
played in the People Power uprising, she encouraged them to urge
the people to follow the nonviolent path of the gospel.

On August 10, 1991 half a million people — with songs, dances and prayers — began a peace march to Ratsiraka's residence, the palace of Iavoloha. No one had planned what to do in case of a violent response. As they neared the palace, the presidential guard, with helicopter support, opened fire. The unarmed people fled, many wounded or killed.

Forces Vives reiterated its determination to continue, and to do so by nonviolent means only. In a letter, Hildegard urged the leaders to try to create an atmosphere that would encourage dialogue and resist those who called for violence. Supported by the Catholic Cardinal Victor Razafimahatrata, other church leaders, and the leaders of the nonviolent resistance, 300,000 attended a night of prayer on October 2.

Ratsiraka's prime minister named as Minister of Defense a general who was sympathetic to the nonviolent movement. The national mood was shifting; at the end of October all ecclesiastical and political representatives gathered for a 48-hour conclave which proposed establishing a caretaker government for eighteen months, to prepare for new elections. The Ecumenical Council representing all the churches, Catholic and Protestant, worked to resolve areas of conflict and disagreement nonviolently (Goss-Mayr, *Wie Feinde* 82ff).

During this critical time of transition, Hildegard made her first visit to Madagascar. Arriving in November she visited the varied programs and met with Cardinal Razafimahatrata, Dr. Zafy, leaders of *Forces Vives,* and with the acting prime minister. She urged the Minister of Defense to maintain the army's neutrality during the coming nonviolent transition. She spoke with religious leaders, theologians, social workers, teachers and students. She also met with many of the grass roots people, destitute and desperate for constructive change. The tapes, articles, films and books by the Goss-Mayrs about their work enhanced the value of these meetings.

Hildegard returned in 1993 with Father Alfred Bour of the French FOR to hold seminars in nonviolence. Madagascar's poverty and other social problems presented a challenge to the new era. But after the seminars, Hildegard observed:

... when we worked on alternatives in the seminars, a wide horizon of initiatives already begun or in the stage of planning opened up: political adversaries worked side by side, schools opened up to the poor carried forward by the unique commitment of teachers, rural cooperatives were created, new methods of cultivation were developed which would not impoverish the soil, education for democracy and personal responsibility was developed. Thanks to the exemplary ecumenical movement in Mahajanga, bishops as well as leading Muslims and Hindus participated in our seminars. This was the fruit of an ecumenical movement which had been practiced for years. Trade unions, NGOs, and people's movements were at work at the base level. If the people, also the poorest, could experience one step forward during this period of government, then a genuine chance for a new life would open up to these people who had suffered so much. (Goss-Mayr, *Wie Feinde* 87)

Hildegard with colleagues from (l. to rt.)
Madagascar, Uganda, Philippines and Hawaii in 2002

10

Interfaith Nonviolence
Across Boundaries

Following the 1986 People Power Revolution in the Philippines, Jean and Hildegard had a rich encounter in Thailand with Buddhist monks, sharing in the transformative power of nonviolence found in both traditions. Christian *agape* — self-giving love — and Buddhist compassion both reach out to the suffering of the oppressed with nonviolent solidarity and action. Together they affirm absolute respect for all humanity.

Leaders like the Vietnamese Zen master Thich Nhat Hanh and his co-worker Chan Chong; the Cambodian monk Maha Gosananda; and the Thai teacher/author Sulak Sivaraksa were developing what came to be known as Engaged Buddhism, a spirituality that includes work for justice, human rights, the environment and peace.

The Goss-Mayrs had based their efforts in nonviolence on their Christian commitment and understanding yet were open to other traditions, especially with the example of Mahatma Gandhi and his multi-faith nonviolent approach to spirituality and liberation. The instance of Buddhist nonviolence they met in a Thai Buddhist monastery offered further evidence of the potential for widening their interreligious work.

A group of Muslims, Hindus, Buddhists and Christians who had been working together in the "Dipshikha" ("spark of light") movement invited them to lead a nonviolence seminar in Bangladesh. Begun by a German priest, Father Klaus, Dipshikha brought rural and village people together in self-help projects — like making handicrafts — so as to affirm values, such as cooperation, honesty, equality, good will, and peace. This movement had particular significance in an impoverished and densely populated nation beset by natural disasters such as seasonal typhoons and floods. Like many other poor nations, Bangladesh has been highly militarized and given to violence.

In this first of a series of seminars, representatives of the various faiths affirmed that their sacred books' absolute respect for the human being provided an antidote to religious fundamentalism, violence and war. The richness of Bengali culture added to the seminars. Worship, for example, used poems set to the music of Rabindranath Tagore, as well as the sacred texts of the various faiths represented. The participants shared their nonviolent struggles for rights — for land and water, for property rights of untouchables, for women — and for reconciliation during the civil war. These experiences led to discussions on the theory and practice of nonviolence and exploring their ancient roots in the Hindu-Buddhist understanding of *ahimsa* — revering all life and refraining from harming any living thing. The Vedas teach that violence is sinful; genuine respect for others makes violence impossible. The eight-fold Buddhist path leads to *ahimsa*, leads to nonviolence. Islam is a religion of universal peace. The Pathan leader Badshah Khan taught, "The Holy Prophet Mohammed came into this world and taught us: 'That man is a Muslim who never hurts anyone by word or deed, but who works for the benefit and happiness of God's creatures. Belief in God is to love one's fellowmen' " (Easwaran 55). Christian nonviolence, rooted in the self-giving love of God as seen in Jesus, has universal meaning and application. In the Sermon on the Mount, Jesus said, "Blessed are the peacemakers, for they shall be called sons of God" (Mt 5:9), and "Love your enemies and pray for those who persecute you, so that you may be sons of your Father who is in heaven; for he makes his sun rise on the evil and the good, and sends rain on the just and on the unjust" (Mt 5:43–45). St. Paul says, "Do not be overcome by evil, but overcome evil with good" (Rm 12:21). The teachings and example of Mahatma Gandhi, who believed in "the infinite possibilities of universal love," provided an inspiring and instructive witness to the interfaith aspects of nonviolence.

After the seminars, Hildegard and Jean met with the Bangladesh Interreligious Council for Peace and Justice and the Catholic Bishops' Conference and attended a lecture at the Dhammarajika Buddhist Monastery and Social Center. A 1988 conference, "Asian Active Nonviolence," presented the broad scope of movements developing in Thailand, the Philippines, Bangladesh and Sri Lanka. These events helped to build a strong interfaith nonviolent presence and witness in Asia and helped to disseminate around the world nonviolence with rich interfaith dimensions.

Beginning in the mid 1970s and continuing into the 2000s, the Goss-Mayrs (and after Jean's death, Hildegard alone) often visited the Middle East. They found ways to develop interfaith and humanist dimensions in the teaching of active nonviolence. After the first and second intifadas, Hildegard helped Israeli and Palestinian Jews, Muslims and Christians prepare a response, including the planning of a peace pilgrimage.

*****

Hildegard sees interfaith developments not as syncretism but rather as a challenge for adherents of each religion to affirm the beauty and depth of their own path, thus preparing the way

> ... to experience the beauty and depth of others. Interaction with the Other is then not a menace but an enrichment. When we reach this state, we will be able to recognize the revelation of God in the other and to accept the gift of their truth.... Only then is it possible to experience unity within diversity as joyful. Only then will we be able to give others their due respect, to invest our energies in the realization of their basic rights, and to accept sharing in Justice. Only then will we begin to cooperate, step by step, in working together in a global project that has the human family at its center. That project will have the aim of establishing a new social

order, building up a responsible relationship with resources, the biosphere, and the cosmos — all this through democratic attitudes and the methods of nonviolence. Utopia? Yes! Because only a person with unequivocal aims, who bears in herself the image of a united, brotherly world — a likeness of the triune God — and believes in it, will find the strength to start upon the toilsome path of drawing nearer to this Utopia, to the realm of God in this world. She will seek and pursue it because in it lies the salvation of humanity. (Goss-Mayr, "Prospects for the Future," 5–6)

Disarmament

A life-long passion to build a disarmed world ran through all of the Goss-Mayr seminars and programs. Modern technology builds ever more lethal weapons that contradict the vision of peace. The development, sale and use of armaments undermine human rights and civil society. The Cold War and its threat of force were used to justify the arms race, yet when the Cold War ended, new reasons were found to continue it.

Jean and Hildegard never ceased making this clear. On June 25, 1988 the Non-Governmental Organizations at the United Nations chose Hildegard to address the General Assembly of the Second Special Session of the United Nations on Disarmament. She told the delegates clearly and forcefully that "there is no way for humanity to become a United Nations, reconciled in justice and peace, other than by passing through the gate of disarmament and constructive peace work." Taking the first three words of the UN Charter, "We the peoples," she spoke movingly of the aim "to create security and life in dignity for all through peaceful means." Spelling this out, she said,

If we are to choose life, we will need those in governmental responsibility to transform their words of peace into deeds of peace. In practice, many governments give little or no attention to mediation, nonviolent action for social justice, disarmament, civil defense and for the application of the Universal Declaration of Human Rights. The entire work of the peace movement has made it clear that it is effectively furthering the founding purposes of the United Nations: to advance international security and peace. By continuing to ignore disarmament, by impeding nonviolent actions and by even imprisoning nonviolent workers, governments permit tensions to escalate irremediably to armed conflict and warfare.

Hildegard concluded with an appeal to the assembled delegates to further the ancient vision of "beating swords into plowshares and spears into pruning hooks" (from an unpublished manuscript by Hildegard Goss-Mayr, UN General Assembly, 1988).

Large-scale peace seminars, fasts and demonstrations were occurring in many countries. At one such gathering Hildegard spoke to seven thousand young people at St. Stephen's Cathedral, Vienna, about the biblical armor that is theirs: "loins girded with truth ... the breastplate of righteousness ... feet shod with the gospel of peace ... the helmet of salvation ... and the sword of the Spirit, which is the word of God" (Eph 6:14–17). Now increasingly recognized as a wise elder of the nonviolent struggle, she reminded them of their true heritage.

In the 1990s and into the new century her addresses have appealed for humanity to "choose life that you and your descendants may live" (Dt 30:19). Drawing upon such events as the Gandhian movement in India, the People Power Revolution in the Philippines, peaceful transitions in Latin America, South Africa and the Soviet bloc of nations, she called upon religious and political entities to train large numbers of people in the work of peace and local, national and international conflict resolution. Both the Vatican and the World Council of Churches recognized her wisdom, experience and scholarship in the field of nonviolence.

At an international conference of the Fellowship of Reconciliation at Manhattan College in New York in 2002, she concluded her address, "Prospects for the Future," with this vision of her patron saint, Hildegard of Bingen:

Humanity stands at the center of the structure of the world.
Although small in stature, humanity is powerful through the
power of its soul. It can set into movement the higher and
the lower things.
Whatever it does with its right or left hand, it penetrates the
Universe.
Because in the strength of the inner person it carries the
ability to do such things.
The power of the soul encompasses the entire world.

(For full article, see pp. 135–40 in this publication)

Hildegard in Compiegne, France, at the consultation planning
the Decade for a Culture of Peace and Nonviolence

11

The Legacy Lives On

The year 1991 was marked by losses. Hildegard and Jean had had residences in both Paris and Vienna, where each had grown up and where they had wide circles of close friends, points of departure and return in their work and travels. After Jean's death, she gave up the apartment in Paris. Later in that fateful year, after a long illness Hildegard's sister, Irene, died. Then, at the end of the year, Hildegard's mother also reached the end of her long and generous life.

Hildegard decided to sell the house in which she had grown up, repository for many years of the Mayr family history. She moved into a small apartment in Vienna owned by the Sisters of Charles Borromeo. From there, she could continue her work and travel, yet be near her children and grandchildren in Vienna and in Strasbourg.

There were also joys in that year of loss. Her daughter Myriam had her fourth child. In recognition of her pioneering interfaith and nonviolent work, Hildegard was awarded the Niwano Peace Prize, an honor given by the Niwano Peace Foundation, Tokyo. This prestigious award — a medal and 20 million yen ($200,000) — allowed her to continue the work — much of it in Africa — to which Jean had given so much of his life. She and Jean had won earlier awards: the Xirinacs Prize for Peace given by Pax Christi Spain in 1976; the Human Rights Prize of Dr. Bruno Kreisky in Vienna in 1979; and the Pope Paul VI Education for Peace Prize of Pax Christi USA in 1986. They were also nominated several times for the Nobel Peace Prize. In 1992 Hildegard and Diana Francis of

England were awarded the Pfeffer Peace Prize of the U.S. Fellowship of Reconciliation. The Pfeffer Prize, presented in Quito, Ecuador at a 1992 world conference, included a cash award and a parchment that noted Hildegard's developing "global connections of interfaith action that witness to the tenacity of her purpose and the impact of her achievements." Archbishop Dom Hélder Câmara once told me, "If the Nobel Peace Prize were mine to give, I would give it to Hildegard and Jean Goss Mayr. They have deeply touched my life." Thomas Merton saw the need for a Catholic training center in nonviolence, and thought Hildegard should direct it. In a letter to William Robert Miller (13 September 1966) Merton wrote that he considered her a candidate for sainthood, "along with Dorothy Day and a few others" (Shannon 252).

Over her many decades of work, funding has come to Hildegard — and before that, to Hildegard and Jean — in a variety of ways. Especially in the early years, the International FOR provided for their financial needs. As their work grew and larger projects developed, so did other sources. Bread for the World and Misereor provided generous support. When Jean once received an inheritance, they used it for their work. Various organizations, religious communities and individuals, especially from Germany and Switzerland, supported them. Over the decades these sources enabled their ministry to spread. Their visionary work required that they raise enough funds to support themselves and their children, to pay a secretary and office expenses, as well as to assist the many projects that developed out of their work. They lived simply and were careful stewards of the funds entrusted to them.

Jean and Hildegard believed that if the funds were lacking, then faith and patience were called for. If the work was authentic and needed, funds would somehow be found.

*****

Hildegard continues her work of writing, workshops and lectures. As the Honorary President of the International Fellowship of Reconciliation and with working relationships with institutions and groups all over the world, she has decided that in her remaining years she would continue to make a special commitment to Africa. That decision was shaped by the combination of widespread human need and international neglect, along with great potential, strong interest, and openings for nonviolent work. Africa had been Jean's passion, where he carried out pioneering work in his final years. She believes that she should continue this important work.

Without doubt, Hildegard has been one of the leading advocates of nonviolence in the twentieth and twenty-first centuries, shaping and guiding humanity's slow but certain discovery of the power of unarmed Truth. Like Gandhi she believes in "the infinite possibilities of universal love." She has been a pioneer and teacher of peace. Her often quiet accomplishments will live on.

Hildegard has witnessed great suffering, violence and injustice throughout the world as well as amazing movements and transformative events. She has sought to approach her life's work with unflagging determination and faith. Typical are these words she and Jean wrote in 1983 in a Christmas letter:

> We should remember that no effort, no action that we carry out through the force of Love and Truth is ever lost. On the contrary, like Jesus who, giving himself away until death, rose to eternal life, in the same way the self-giving force of Love with which we commit ourselves is THE POWER that overcomes injustice even if we do not see immediate results! It is the force of Life, the force of renewal in society, the liberating force of humanity.

Articles by
Hildegard Goss-Mayr

"First, never kill;
second, never hurt;
third, commit yourself incessantly
and with perseverance;
fourth, remain always united;
fifth, disobey the orders of the authorities
that violate or destroy us."

Principles of the peasants of Alagamar
in their nonviolent struggle for land reform

Filipinos stopping a tank during the People Power Revolution in the Philippines (from *People Power: An Eyewitness History*. Permission from James B. Reuter, S.J.)

Jean and Hildegard Goss-Mayr with President Corazon Aquino of the Philippines

Alagamar: Nonviolent Land Struggle

In most Latin American countries military or civilian dictator-ships, on the basis of the doctrine of national security, continue to uphold an economic system of exploitation that favors a small group of privileged individuals (as well as national and multina-tional enterprises in the First World) and condemns the vast ma-jority of the people to a life of dependence, misery, and political and social marginalization. But the masses of the poor in Latin America have increasingly become aware of their human rights and dignity, and in many parts of the continent, despite violent and brutal repression, they have begun to organize and struggle for change. Popular civic movements are springing up and press-ing for justice.

Within this process, the Christian Churches carry considerable responsibility. Based on decisions taken by the Latin American Bishops' Conference in 1968 in Medellin and confirmed in 1979 in Puebla, the Catholic Church considers it her mission to take a firm stand on the side of the poor. There are great differences as to the degree of commitment among Christians and Church leader-ship. The current within the Church favoring the status quo and a modus vivendi with the established forces has grown in strength during the past few years. Yet Christians in many Latin American countries — peasants, workers, pastoral workers, priests, bishops, young people, women and men — have committed themselves in the struggle for basic justice and human rights, even to the point of giving their lives. The Latin American Church has become a Church of martyrs.

While many people understand that fidelity to the gospel requires an identification with the poor and exploited, certainly not all of them have come to see that the liberating force of the gospel (what Dom Hélder Câmara has called the "radically new message" capable of breaking through the spiral of domination of man over man) is the power of nonviolence. These people base their commitment, in the last resort, on the old doctrine, still kept alive in our Churches, of the "just war," of "just revolutionary and insurrectional violence" — with all its consequences of destruction of lives, values, human relationships and of a political and a social nature.

However, there also exists a deep current, mainly among the poor in the Christian grassroots communities (*communidades de base*) and among the indigenous population, strengthened and nourished by certain Church leaders, which in its liberation struggle wants to remain faithful in a radical way to the gospel and refuses the oppressors' provocation to violence. It refuses hatred and counter-violence in the process of struggling for a truly fraternal and just society.

This current is particularly important in Brazil. There, eighteen years ago, some 900 workers of the cement factory of "Perus," with the assistance of the lawyer Mario Carvalho de Jesus, started out on a strike to obtain basic workers rights [see *IFOR Report,* December 1978]. This was the first outspokenly nonviolent campaign in Brazil. It lasted seven years and set precedents on many fronts: law and jurisdiction, solidarity among the working class, and challenges to the Church, intellectuals, and the middle class. The cost of the strike was torture, imprisonment, and even the life of one participant who died of hunger.

The success of "Perus" was not primarily the money paid to the workers when they won their strike, but a first deep awareness that the people, the poor and exploited who unite in a commitment to justice, possess the power of nonviolence which is capable of overcoming injustice.

Awareness of this nonviolent liberating force of the gospel also sprang up among a handful of Church leaders, bishops like Dom

Hélder Câmara, Jose Maria Pires, Dom Fragoso, Cardinal Arns and Cardinal Lorscheider. They began to bring it to life in their pastoral work. They also carried it with strong faith into the Brazilian Catholic Bishops' Conference, trying gradually to unite and transform it into an instrument of nonviolent liberation on the side of the poor during the height of military dictatorship. Although this commitment was never joined by all the bishops, nevertheless, during the hardest time of repression in the '70s, the Church of Brazil was a strong pillar on the side of the poor and defenseless. It took stands for the protection of political prisoners, the indigenous and the landless, for general amnesty, for basic democratic rights and for a new and just economical order. It accepted to pay the price for its commitment by refusing all former privileges and positions of power.

At the same time, this work for liberation with the power of the gospel grew and was made concrete in many of the thousands of Christian grassroots communities that sprang up throughout the country. At the moment, due to a certain political and democratic opening, civic, popular movements are strengthening. Grassroots communities are like a yeast in this struggle. Thus the big metal workers' strike of the past year, the movement for amnesty for political prisoners, the movement against the high cost of living, etc., have been very largely nonviolent, characterized by an attitude of wisdom and constraint, refusing the provocation to counter-violence.

At present the battle for land is one of the hardest and most tragic problems of Brazil. Millions of rural workers and peasants have been chased from the land they tilled and on which they and their families lived. Big national and international firms are moving in. Intermediaries with armed private police threaten the poor or indigenous people and drive them away by force, acting unpunished, protected by those in power, and against the laws of the country, in particular the agrarian reform laws. While in some areas, specifically in the Amazonian basin, the poor are repeatedly resorting to counter-violence (with the poor means at their disposal) in order to defend their life and rights, in the northeast of Brazil, and particularly in the diocese of Archbishop Jose Maria Pires of Joao Pessoa, the peasants are becoming more and more united in a nonviolent liberating struggle for the land. Alagamar is an example.

Due to the need to produce sugar for alcohol to be added to gasoline (part of Brazil's program in response to increasing oil prices), the value of land in the area of Alagamar has increased tremendously. Big companies wanting to profit from the sugar cane boom try to get hold of the land and throw off the peasants.

Christian grassroots communities are strongly developed in the area. For these Christians, the struggle for justice is inseparably linked to their faith. Thus, when a new proprietor took over and wanted them to submit to his orders, the peasants of Alagamar immediately consulted a lawyer at the "Center for the Defense of Human Rights" of the diocese, to find out about their rights. The answer was clear: according to the law, the land they tilled was theirs. Measures of the owner to expel them would be unlawful. They decided to resist.

This decision was made in a large mud hut, which the peasants have built to serve as their chapel and community meeting place. The very fact that they met, prayed, and discussed their problems was seen by the owner as a dangerous, subversive act. One day when the men had gone to the market, his private police came and destroyed the chapel. It was like a warning: do not dare to resist!

The news of the destruction spread quickly. The following Sunday the priest of the area and Archbishop Jose Maria Pires celebrated the Eucharist in the destroyed chapel, with several hundred peasants attending. Public opinion began to be stirred up.

Step by step solidarity and unity began to develop, drawing in small communities and more and more peasants of the area, the Church, and eventually people of the town.

The peasants tried to negotiate with the owner but never succeeded. Therefore they decided to take their case to court and to try to win the agricultural unions and the regional land reform authorities to their side. They knew a long struggle lay ahead. As they continued their efforts repression stiffened. They were spied upon, slandered, cheated, and interrogated by the police.

When, because of their actions, some of them were arrested and taken to town the peasants decided they were all equally responsible. Hundreds marched to town and filled up the house of the judge, demanding to join those who had been arrested. Finally the judge was obliged to send them all home, including the prisoners.

In order to sustain their struggle financially they began to plant collective fields of manioc. One day, as some eighty of them were working on one of these fields, the owner sent armed men to tear up the plants and destroy the harvest.

This was a tremendous challenge. The eighty peasants got together and discussed what to do, reminding themselves of the principles Dom Jose Maria had elaborated with them: "First, never kill; second, never hurt; third, remain always united; ..." They decided to resist the provocation to counter-violence. Silently they watched the men tearing up three thousand plants!

The next day they went into the field and planted them anew. The Archbishop came to the spot, picked up some of the uprooted plants, and took them to town to place on the cathedral altar. To the whole diocese he appealed: "These peasants are truly living the nonviolent liberating power of the gospel. Let us follow their example and sustain their just combat!"

People's minds began to change. The question arose: Who is "subversive," the peasants who with peaceful means try to apply the laws of the country in order that justice may be achieved for all, or the firm that steals from the poor their small and last resources?

Solidarity grew, pressure increased. On the occasion of the visit of the President of the Republic to Joao Pessoa, 2,500 hectares of land (out of 10,000 in dispute) were handed over to the people. And the struggle is continuing.

(*IFOR Report*, July 1980, pp. 14–16)

The Women of Medellin

In 1968, during our working tour of South America, my husband Jean and I visited Colombia. We were grieved both by the poverty and by the hardened detachment of the Colombian Church. Yet among the young priests, we found many who took up the cause of the poor. One of them was Padre Gabriel, who had developed Christian base communities among about 7,000 poor peasants in the slums of Barrio Santo Domingo in Medellin.

With the help of friends, Gabriel had prepared a seminar on active nonviolence, in which Jean and I took part. The residents of the barrio offered us lodging. People came from Colombia, Peru, Panama, Venezuela, Bolivia, and Ecuador. We held our meetings in the common house, which the residents had built of clay. Every evening many of them visited us, and we shared our feelings about the day's work. Then they read texts from the Bible and interpreted them in the perspective of their life struggle.

In small groups we worked out strategies for the fight in the barrio and elsewhere. On the last evening, when each person was invited to give his or her personal witness, a union leader said to us: "My house is your house. Come back soon. We are alone. I was a guerrilla and lost fifteen members of my family. Then I became a soldier and, to my own shame, I shot at my fellow citizens.... Today I am convinced that the true power of the poor is nonviolence. I see future leaders among us. The fight will be hard, and they will try to kill us. But the people will love us, because they have only one wish, and that is to be freed from misery and fear and no longer to be surrounded by death. Let us begin!"

During the weeks and months following the nonviolence seminar, the people of the barrio began to act. About a hundred women came together to achieve what they needed most urgently: the laying of pipes for drinking water. First they tried to engage the city administration in dialogue. However, the distance between the slums and the powerful city council was too great. The women of the barrio had no influence: they received only empty promises. So they decided to appeal to the consciences of wealthy women, in gestures that expressed their need.

The women came together in groups of ten, took their smallest children, and went down to the elegant town square. There, a huge fountain spilled clear water into a pool day and night. The wind blew water over the rim and left puddles on the ground. The first group of women went up to the fountain and began to bathe their children, not in the pool but in the puddles. Immediately, women of the upper class stopped and challenged the women of the barrio. "You stupid things, your children will die if you wash them in that dirty water!" Now the women could give witness about their problem: the lack of drinking water, the denial of the city authorities, and the deaths among their children. But the police came immediately and drove the women away.

A few minutes later, a second group arrived. They made the same protest gestures and held discussions with a growing number of wealthy persons — a signal for the police to step in, threatening to make arrests. After a few minutes, a third group came and repeated the action. The number of women of the upper class gathering around the fountain grew even larger. Then a policeman attacked the poor women with a club. A lady stopped him. "Señor, if your wife were in this situation, wouldn't you fight for drinking water too?"

Solidarity had succeeded. The protest of the barrio women had stirred an echo in the place where most women are vulnerable: where the lives and deaths of their children are at stake. They had brought the struggle to the level of the conscience. They had built their hopes on the conviction that wealthy women, confronted with the power of truth, are capable of opening their hearts; that they are open to new insights; that their consciences can grow and widen.

On that same day, women from both classes of the population formed a committee. They held negotiations with the city administration. Now that the inequality of power had been overcome, dialogue was possible. Men from the barrio volunteered to lay the water pipes: several months later, drinking water flowed from the spigot on the mountain. A first small step had been taken.

The women had tried the strength of nonviolence and had experienced growth through it, and were emboldened to continue their fight. The Church, however, remained aligned with those in power. They prohibited Padre Gabriel's "subversive" work in the barrio and drove him out.... Today Medellin is the center of the drug mafia!

(*Fellowship,* "Nonviolence in the Arena,"
March/April 2000, p. 23, taken from Hildegard Goss-Mayr,
Making Friends of Enemies)

Hildegard in 2002 at the IFOR Conference
at Manhattan College in New York City

Propositions on Christian Peace for Schema 17 of The Second Vatican Council

C hrist the Lord is the Prince of Peace[1] coming in the fullness of the times[2] to give his life as a ransom for the lives of many[3] according to the will of the Father who sent Him.[4] Our peace is therefore Christ Himself, who in reconciling all men to God through his cross and restoring the unity of all in one people and one body has killed hatred in his own flesh.[5] Thus has He proclaimed peace to all men and all nations.[6] All Christians, and indeed all men, are called to build up more perfectly this peace of Christ every day, since through the coming of Christ we are now in the time of salvation[7] and the last hour.[8] The form and effect of this peace is that earthly peace proceeding from a true love of neighbor, a love which does no evil and is the fulfillment of the Law.[9] By living truth in love,[10] all Christians are obliged to contribute throughout the whole world to the creation of the conditions of love and justice, without which there can be no true peace.

The spirit of Christ the Lord is indeed the spirit of meekness (*mansuetude*) and humility,[11] renouncing violence,[12] opposed by nature to force even in its just use,[13] seeking — by a love embracing even enemies[14] — to overcome evil with good.[15] There can be no doubt therefore that the killing of one's neighbor — even in a just war or otherwise caused without injustice — is contrary to Christian meekness (*lenitas*).[16] For that reason those whose personal vocation is genuinely shown to be the procuring and exercising of the peace of Christ in a more perfect way, legitimately refuse those services in which, by their own nature, the killing of one's neighbor has an essential place.

Moreover in our present age it is extremely difficult to fulfill the conditions required for a just war and often impossible for citizens to judge with sufficient probability about the justness of a particular war.[17] Nevertheless in the final consideration of conscience this judgment cannot be surrendered to the civil authorities. Furthermore in modern war it is very often impossible for soldiers to control an act of war by keeping it within the moral limits of their own actions. Since all these things are true, the right order of reason and nature itself demand that those whose conscience tells them to refuse military service must not be forced to take up arms.

In this regard, total war, which employs every means of injuring an enemy that seems (or which can seem in the war itself) effective and necessary for victory, is gravely unjust and contrary to charity. Total war admits even those methods which involve the direct and deliberate taking of innocent human life, inasmuch as they are directed at the destruction of the innocent as the means to an end which may be licit in itself, as a desired victory. For these reasons total war is gravely illicit in any hypothesis whatsoever (cfr. Pius XII, Alloc. d. 29.10.1951, 838).

It is therefore necessary to reject as shameful the use of any instrument of war which bears with it so great an evil that it cannot be controlled by man, which is to say that the effect of the means employed is by its very nature the total annihilation of human life within the radius of such an action, in which necessarily even the innocent are found. For in this case the total efficacy of the weapon employed is certainly the means of obtaining the destruction of the enemy forces. Thus the annihilation of all life, of even the innocent, is employed precisely as the means of obtaining victory (cfr. Pius XII; Alloc. d. 30.9.1954, AAS 46, 1954, 589).

(Part of the text developed by Jean and Hildegard Goss-Mayr with Karl Rahner, Bernard Häring and Yves Congar, included in *Gaudium et Spes* Vol. II, Chap 5.)

Notes

1. Is. 9:4-6.
2. Eph. 1:13.
3. Mt. 20:28.
4. Io. 6:38; Eph. 1:5.
5. Eph. 2:14-16.
6. Eph. 2:17; Is. 57:19; Zach. 9:10.
7. 2 Cor. 6:2.
8. 1 Io. 2:18.
9. Rom. 13:10.
10. Eph. 4:15.
11. Mt. 11:29.
12. Mt. 26:52; Lk. 9:54-56.
13. Mt. 5:38-42.
14. Mt. 5:43-48.
15. Rom. 12:17-21.
16. Cfr. Decr. Grat. C.5., c.6. D 501, c.1, c.4, c.5, D511 c.29, c.30 C XXIII, q.81 et C.C.C. c.984.
17. All Catholics should bear seriously in mind the theological doctrine which lays down the conditions for a just war.

When Prayer and Revolution Became People Power

We know that not one step, not one seed, not one action that is carried out in the spirit of nonviolence is ever lost. It bears fruit, in the history of nations and of the world. But even though we know this, it is encouraging and helpful to be able to see the practical results of nonviolent action from time to time. That is why I would like to share with you some of the things that happened in the Philippines during the recent liberation struggle, although — I should like to add immediately — it is only a first step in the struggle for a life of dignity for all Filipinos.

The international press has covered it quite well, but there are aspects of what the people of the Philippines lived through that very few journalists have been able to grasp. The press could not relate the events that occurred to the traditions and the attitudes of the people that made them possible.

Nonviolence — this power of truth and love — always develops out of a given historical and cultural background. The Filipino people were under Spanish domination for three centuries, and a US colony for half a century. Later on, during the Second World War, they were occupied by the Japanese and liberated by the Americans. While the US did not set up another colonial regime, it established a strong military presence in the Philippines and made that country economically dependent upon the multinational firms.

Three centuries of Spanish rule brought Christianity to the Philippines, leaving behind, as in Latin America, a mostly Catholic country in the Spanish tradition. It is important to understand that the majority of the Filipino people are a believing people, with a faith like that of children, but not in a negative sense, at all. Our children often have a very close relationship to God. There is no theology in between. Many Filipino people are like those in Latin America who have said to me, "God has spoken into my ear, He said this and this." Sometimes the gospel comes directly into the hearts and minds of the people, in a way that is not rationalized, as it is in other countries.

More recently, there was almost twenty years of the Marcos regime with the suffering of the people increasing, seen in unemployment, hunger, and misery.

Whenever groups in some of the dioceses began to form in the struggle for justice, repression set in immediately. Very great atrocities were committed. This repression came down upon the peasants, students, labor unions and committed Christians. Only a small part of the Church opted to stand on the side of the people and work for social justice. There were perhaps some thirty dioceses where Christian Base Communities were formed.

Bishop Claver in Mindanao was one of the first to develop nonviolent liberating actions in his diocese. Some of the sisters and priests were persecuted, but the majority of the Church leadership and most of the middle class were linked to the regime. As in Latin America, the Church as an official institution was linked to those in power much too long. It is easy to understand why idealistic young people — seminarians and lay people alike — saw no other way out but to join the guerrillas. Known as the New People's Army (or the NPA), they were established as the armed branch of the Communist Party, more or less on a Maoist basis. These young people saw no other way to struggle for justice against an unjust regime. I think the Church must bear a large part of the responsibility for the development, due to the cowardice of large sections of the official Church.

People cannot remain passive under certain circumstances. Unless there is the offer of a nonviolent alternative, they will have to take to counter-violence. Gandhi has said that the lowest possible attitude is to remain passive; if you don't know another way, you choose counter-violence. This is not to defend counter-violence, but I think it is a reality of which we must be aware. Wherever the moral authorities — whether it be Christian churches or other moral authorities — do not take the lead in nonviolent resistance there will be counter-violence and, sooner or later, civil war. I think we should understand this, and never condemn those who join the guerrillas because they see no other way. But we must try to live that alternative.

Another important event in the Philippine story was the assassination of Ninoy Aquino. This opposition leader had been imprisoned for seven years when he became very ill and had to be operated on in the US. It may not be well known that while he was in prison Ninoy Aquino underwent a radical change, a kind of conversion. He was certainly an honest person, but like all politicians he had been trying to get power. While in prison, he read the gospel and Gandhi and began to understand that a politician must serve the people. He decided then that if he ever had the chance to assume responsibility for his country, he would try to be a politician who worked with nonviolence and served the people rather than himself. It is important to understand that this man, who sought leadership in a country where corruption among the political and economic leaders was a way of life, underwent a deep conversion.

When Ninoy Aquino returned to the Philippines in 1983 he knew he had been condemned to death. When he stepped off the plane and was shot to death, his act of courage in returning held great meaning for the Filipinos. They saw him, as we say in the Old Testament, as a "just one," who gives his life for the people, rather than take the life of the enemy. And we also know from the early Church that the blood of the martyr is fruitful; it has the strength to renew people, to bring a challenge and change those who are passive, or those who are collaborative with the dictatorship. Ninoy's giving the gift of his life was really the beginning of a strong popular effort in the Philippines to try to overcome the dictatorship through nonviolence. Following the assassination, demonstrations began to take place all over the Philippines. The fact that one person had the courage to give his life encouraged thousands and thousands of others to overcome the fear that had kept them passive. They poured into the streets to witness to truth and justice, and to demand that martial law be discontinued and human rights respected.

The demonstrations lasted for months, but there was no ongoing nonviolent action; people were not yet prepared for that. Polarization increased; repression became fierce; and the economic situation continued to deteriorate. NPA actions were on the increase in two-thirds of the provinces of the Philippines.

It was then that a few religious communities wrote to Jean and me, asking if we would come just to study the situation and see whether there might be the possibility of developing a well-organized, coherent nonviolent resistance to the existing injustice. We thought perhaps our Latin American experience might help us understand the Philippine situation, so we accepted. We went to the Philippines for the first time in February 1984. With the help of religious sisters and priests, we traveled throughout the islands and met many people: people close to the regime, people in opposition, peasants, lay people, union leaders, priests, bishops and politicians.

Jean and I felt that we were coming into the situation with nonviolence at a very late hour. I think we must say to our shame that we all close our eyes for a long time in the face of injustice. Very often those who see no other way than counter-violence are the first ones to take action against injustice. It is very difficult to come in later and say no, we should take another path. We Christians should be the first ones to open our eyes to injustices, and to speak out and bring the power of nonviolence into the revolution. We felt it was late, but we felt that there were people really searching for the nonviolent alternative.

One thing that made us decide to accept the challenge was when, on the last day of our first visit, the brother of Ninoy Aquino — he's called Agapito ("Butz") Aquino — came to see us. He said to Jean and me: "A few days ago, we were approached by arms merchants, who said, 'Do you think you will be able to overthrow this regime with demonstrations? Don't you think you need better weapons than that? We're offering them to you. Make up your mind.' " And then he said to us: "It is providential that you have come at this time, because ever since their visit I have been unable to sleep. Do I have the right to throw my country into a major civil war? What is my responsibility as a Christian politician in this situation? Is there really such a thing as nonviolent combat against a system as unjust as this one?" Jean and I told him that at least he could try. "You don't lose anything if you try with nonviolence," we said. "But you must make up your own mind, and if you decide to try it, you must prepare yourself inwardly, because nonviolent methods are the fruit of the vision of man that we have. If you want to have seminars in preparation, let us know, and we will come back."

A few weeks later, we were invited back to carry out a series of seminars on nonviolent liberation. One of these seminars was with the group of bishops that had already committed itself to working for social justice. Bishop Claver had organized a seminar for them. The others were mainly for leaders from the political opposition, for labor unions, peasants, students and church people — priests, sisters and lay people.

In each of these seminars we would first analyze the situation of violence together, and how we were a part of it. The seed of the violence was in structures, of course, and in the dictator. But wasn't it also in ourselves? It's very easy to say that Marcos is evil. But unless we each tear the dictator out of our own heart, nothing will change. Another group will come into power and will act similarly to those whom they replaced. So we discovered the Marcos within ourselves.

In some of these seminars there were political leaders of the opposition, and there were peasant leaders. In one seminar, the peasants would not speak to the politicians. "We have no faith in the politicians," they said. "Even if they are from the opposition, they have betrayed us too often." So one evening when we celebrated the Eucharist together, Father Jose Blanco, a Jesuit priest, distributed the host immediately after consecration. "Let us now break the bread," he said, "and bring one part of the host to someone with whom you have not yet talked during our seminar." There was a deep silence. Finally one person from the labor unions got up, walked up to one of the political leaders present, and shared his host with him. Deeply moved, the politician promised that if he got the chance of political leadership, he would firmly stand on the side of the poor. This was the breakthrough: unity was achieved. This unity is the pre-condition for nonviolent liberation work. Those seminars were more than just training people in methodology. The goal was for each one of us to undergo a deep change, a conversion.

The nonviolent movement of the Philippines, called AKKAPKA, developed out of these seminars, under the leadership of Father

Blanco. AKKAPKA is Tagalog for "I embrace you," as well as an acronym for Movement for Peace and Justice. Everybody who took part in a seminar was asked to pass on what they had learned, what they had experienced. And during the first year AKKAPKA was in existence, those few people held forty seminars in thirty provinces of the Philippines. They saw an urgent need to share what they had learned, so that the people might be prepared, at least to some extent, for non-violent change in the country.

When the so-called "snap" elections were announced at the end of 1985, AKKAPKA discontinued the training to work at preparing for the electoral process. They encouraged people to have the courage to vote for the person whom they really believed should be the leader in the country, and to refuse to accept the money that was offered by the government for Marcos votes. They prepared people to defend the ballot-boxes. Young and old, men and women, priests and lay people stood unarmed around the urns that held the ballots in the face of armed agents who came to steal them.

AKKAPKA also decided that from the middle of January to the end of the struggle, they would have "prayer tents." One tent was set up right in the banking center in Manila, where the financial power of the regime was concentrated. This big prayer tent was set up there in a little park. And around it, people who promised to fast and pray had a presence day and night. We cannot emphasize enough the deep spirituality that gave the people the strength to stand against the tanks later on. People prayed every day, for all those who suffered in the process of changing regimes, even for the military, and for Marcos: that he would find the strength not to use his huge arsenal against the people — that what little love for his people that was perhaps left in his heart might prevent him from giving the order to shoot into the millions of people who were demonstrating.

It makes a great difference, in a revolutionary process where people are highly emotional, whether you promote hatred and revenge or help the people stand firmly for justice without becoming like the oppressor. You want to love your enemy, to liberate rather than destroy him.

Radio Veritas, the Catholic station, helped tremendously in this task. It coordinated the whole resistance, around the clock, with news of the events as they happened. Day and night, they read passages from Martin Luther King, the Sermon on the Mount, Gandhi, and so forth — asking the people to follow those examples. Radio Veritas also encouraged the soldiers to remember their vow of loyalty to the nation, and not to one person. They kept urging the troops "Refuse to shoot at the people, on whose side you should stand. Refuse unjust orders."

To do all this in a situation where the dictatorship was still powerful was more than human courage. It was marvelous to see the atmosphere in which it all took place, where prayer and revolution had become one. The revolutionary effort was really a revolution of the strength of truth and love. This is why, in the midst of it all, people were able to sing and dance. They knew they had a strength within them that was stronger than their own little human strength, that the power of love and truth was carrying them along. Therefore, while they were afraid, they knew at the same time that victory was possible. Because truth is stronger than lying, and love is stronger than the hatred and the repression of the regime, it will win in the end.

Now I should like to say a word about Cory Aquino, because it seems like a miracle that this nation was able to unite in so short a time. One factor was certainly the deep suffering the people shared. Their suffering and their faith united them. But I think the pole around whom everything revolved was Cory Aquino. In the eyes of the people, she represented the opposite of all the corruption, oppression and violence of Marcos. When the Filipino people united around Cory Aquino, I think it was because they felt the authenticity of this woman.

In the end, there were only two pillars of the regime left. One was the United States, which gave its support to the Marcos government until the very last moment. And one was the army. While we were there last year, with Cory Aquino, Cardinal Sin and the others, a number of scenarios of possible conflicts that might evolve in the struggle were developed. The scenario everybody feared the most was that the army would split. We knew that if the army split, a great deal of blood would be shed. We had to ask ourselves what could be done if this should happen. That was, in fact, the scenario that evolved. When the reform movement of the army separated from Marcos, he gave the order to his armed forces to crush the dissidents. As planned, Radio Veritas immediately called upon the people to fill up the streets, to stand in front of the tanks, to speak to the soldiers. Eventually there were several hundred thousand people who spent a whole weekend in the road, blocking the tanks so that they could not move against the dissident groups. They spoke to the soldiers, gave them flowers, hugged them, and said, "You belong to the people; come back to those to whom you really belong."

While it was very important for the people to experience the strength of the poor and the power of love and truth to overcome evil, we all know it is only the first step. What is before the Filipino people now is at least as difficult, if not more difficult, than what has gone before. It will require perseverance. And it will need the continued conversion of those who still adhere to the old regime, who have important places in the provinces; to dismantle the private armies of the landlords; to carry out land reform so that the mass of the people can live in dignity; to negotiate with the Muslim minority; to negotiate with the NPA, so that perhaps they will be willing to put down their arms and become one of the democratic parties in the country to rebuild the economy.

It is important that we do not forget Cory Aquino and those who support her, and that our prayers accompany her. We must also encourage our own governments to give economic and moral support to this new government. Not the kind of economic support that makes the Philippines dependent upon others, but economic support that will enable the Philippines to realize its own model of economy and its own model of social reforms.

The nonviolent revolution in the Philippines comes to us as a great gift. It has given hope to countries like Chile, South Korea and others where there are still dictatorships. Perhaps the peace movement, where we have experienced a little bit of what the strength of God in the poor can mean, can also receive this gift, if we really believe in it and if we act accordingly.

(Hildegard Goss-Mayr, *Fellowship* [March 1987], pp. 8-11)

On Liberation Theology

We lived in Latin America when liberation theology was first evolving, and I believe that on several points it has an essential message. One is that you have to know your situation and then you must ask yourself how the work of God helps you to find an answer in this situation.

We have known many people who joined the guerrillas because they saw no other way. And we have to be very honest and say that this reflects a failing in Catholic theology, because we have not properly taught the radical message of nonviolence. Liberation theology took the very important step of seeing that you have to identify with those who suffer. But then some theologians stopped there. In the question of means, they remained with the old Just War theology, which is still alive and well in the West.

This is where the work of the nonviolent movement is important, when it says we should try to find the means that correspond with the message of Jesus. Here, as in so many ways, it has been the poor who have taught the theologians. In reading the Bible, they encountered new strength; in the story of Israel's liberation from slavery, they have discovered their own story.

They would say to their comrades, "You have to learn how to say no to the government, even if it costs you." It was really a conversion that was necessary, inside the people. Not to lie, not to steal, and not to kill. Very simple. And yet, when it comes, it is a source of terrific strength. It brings a spirit of joy because people feel that real life is springing up.

In the Philippine revolution, the atmosphere of coordinated nonviolent action reflected a deep spirituality. The people believed that there is a strength of truth, which is the strength of God, and their prayer and commitment had an impact on the situation.

(Hildegard Goss-Mayr, writing in January 1987 in *World Ministry News*, the newsletter of the Madison [WS] Urban Ministry. Reprinted in *Fellowship* [March 1987], p. 11)

Violent and Nonviolent Revolution

The question is one that has been discussed many times and will continue to be discussed as long as nonviolent forms of revolution (or radical transformation, or whatever name you choose) are so little developed, so little known and taught, and so little practiced as they are now. In many cases not only political but religious leaders still teach "justified violence" and do nothing to help men and women to learn and experience the truly liberating strength of deeply-rooted, organized, active nonviolence. It is not surprising that so many people, in their desperation and in response to the violence they experience each day, opt for violent combat — and in this we who are convinced of nonviolence must respect their conscience. But at the same time we have to look closely at the situations where violence has been chosen, and to remind others of these situations: in El Salvador there have been five years of slaughter and it can go on for ages, Lebanon has now experienced ten years of mutual slaughter, and in Nicaragua the violence and counter-violence are hardening the lines of division within the country. We see again that there is an inseparable link between means and ends. Violent means, even when used with the best intentions, create new forms of violence. Also we must point out how the big powers make use of "small" guerrilla violence for their own purposes. To break out of this vicious cycle new ways and means have to be invented that carry the seed of human respect. In this we bear the new society within ourselves. We in our movement are asked to carry this alternative to humankind and into history with its permanent need for change, but also with its need for a means of change that does not cause dehumanization or threaten destruction. We must be the leaven of these changes, going right into the midst of conflict, willing to go the way of suffering to reach greater justice, liberating the oppressed and the oppressor, or otherwise there will be no real, lasting change. Counter-revolution will begin immediately, nourished by the "big brothers" of the super powers.

In 1964, when Jean and I were living in Brazil, it was the year of the military coup. The situation was dramatic and all seemed lost. Many turned to armed resistance which became the movement of the "city guerrilla," soon crushed by the military in a wave of terror and torture. We were able to help in the building of a nonviolent alternative in Brazil. Of course this issue of violence and nonviolence was under constant discussion. In this largely Christian country, this also required profound reflection on what it means having been baptized in the name of Jesus, to bring into the revolutionary process the liberating power that we are charged as disciples to apply in history, in the time and place where we are living. All this was twenty years ago, and now we can see some positive results of what happened then. But the debate about violence and nonviolence is certainly not finished.

(Hildegard Goss-Mayr, *Reconciliation International*
[February 1986], p. 8)

Active Nonviolence:
A Creative Power for
Peacemaking and Healing

To respect more authentically human life and the whole of creation we need to remind ourselves of the inspiration and driving force of this commitment: *the power of nonviolence as it is revealed to us in the Bible and particularly in Jesus Christ.* We see it in action as a *liberating, healing, and peacemaking force* in the life of people and nations.

We are living in the age of globalization. The process of *globalization* contains both *negative and positive* aspects:

Negative Challenges

Since the end of Communism in the early '90s of the past century, *liberal capitalism,* a materialistic economic system, has gained global influence and domination. Many millions of people suffer from the consequences of this ideology and economic system. Its aim is profit and power. Mankind must serve it. In the hard competition the small ones fall by the wayside. The weak and underqualified are marginalized, subsisting in poverty or even misery. World-wide economic domination is also secured by military force. This holds particularly true for the developing countries. To point out just one example: the Democratic Republic of Congo suffered the loss of over two million people in the recent war over its resources of gold, diamonds and coltan, needed for space engines. This war was supported by seven African nations and transnational enterprises of the North. Or we should remind ourselves of the recent wars over the access to reserves of oil in the Sudan, in Afghanistan or — perhaps tomorrow — in Iraq. The resources of the earth and its environment are exploited to the point of provoking a global ecological collapse (e.g., the pollution of water and air, dramatic climatic changes, deforestation, advance of the deserts, etc.). Hunger, illiteracy, mass unemployment, migration and also terrorism are consequences of this situation.

This dramatic reality forces us to search for *a new vision of the relationship between humankind, God, and all of creation, that is to say, a Shalom vision.*

Positive Challenges

To me it is fundamental to recognize and welcome this development towards global unity. Never before have there existed technical instruments like the internet that permit people all over the world to establish contacts, communicate information, exchange discoveries, provide knowledge and insights. Relief programs in case of accidents and catastrophies can be quickly organized. Sports, art, and particularly music from all continents and cultures converge and can help to build a global human family. The increasing importance of international NGOs and of organizations of the United Nations like UNESCO, WHO and UNICEF provide powerful support to regions in need, and progress has been made in the development and application of international law. Also the peace movement is profiting from modern means of communication to build global networks and give support to endangered groups. It is the project of God, the Creator, for humanity to move towards what Teilhard de Chardin calls the Omega point, that is, the point when the whole creation will be united in love. There is a deep desire for this unity in mankind: it finds expression in the concepts of Shalom (Judaism), of Umma (Islam), of Harmony (Asian religions and philosophies), of a world society without classes and poverty (in Marxism), in the concept of self-giving love and brotherhood (in Christianity).We are called upon to work actively for this end.

Universal ethics promoted by world religions: World religions can help to lead the way to the acceptance of ethics based upon *universally affirmed values*, in spite of the fact of their being presently abused in a scandalous way by fundamentalist concepts for power politics, violence, terrorism and war in all of the world religions. In order to fulfill this task, however, world religions have to return to their deepest roots to rediscover and affirm those values that are required for humane togetherness. These values include in particular: *the absolute respect for human life, commitment for justice and human rights, the use of nonviolent means of overcoming injustices and violence, forgiveness, and the search for reconciliation.* Let me quote from the experience of a seminar on nonviolence in Bangladesh organized by the nonviolent movement *Dipshika* with Muslims, Hindus, Buddhists and Christians.

Our *Muslim* friends pointed out:

When God created humanity to be vice-regents on earth, his Spirit entered every man, woman and child, for He says: "When I have fashioned him and breathed into him My Spirit, fall you down in obeisance to him" (Surate 15/29). In this sense humanity is one. Human life is sacred. "And if anyone saves a life, it would be as if he saved the life of the whole people" (5/35).

Our *Hindu* friends pointed out:

Swami Vivekananda said: "In this world the human body is the supreme body and man is the highest creature. Nobody is beyond man." He reminded us of their offerings to the Supreme and of the renunciation of the will to destroy or to hurt others. Gandhi's Ahimsa seeks not only to overcome the practice of violence but even the intention to do harm to others.

Buddhist participants explained that they are deeply committed to liberation of the powers that cause suffering and deprive people of their value; that their faith is based on unconditional respect for any living being and insisted upon these words from the Buddha: "In those who harbor thoughts of vengeance towards others, hatred will never cease.... For hatred is never appeased by hatred. It is appeased by love. This is an eternal law. Let one's thoughts of boundless love pervade the whole world ... without any obstruction, without any hatred or enmity."

Rabbis for Human Rights in Israel would add: "What is hateful to you, do not do to others" (Hillel). "When a stranger resides with you in your land he shall be to you as one of your citizens" (Lv 19:33). We beat our swords into plows (see Is 2:4).

But those of us who are *Christians* are challenged in particular to be pathfinders for these convictions and this commitment. If we do not return to the Sermon on the Mount and place ourselves clearly and consistently on the side of the poor, and if we do not demand their rights to be respected in politics and economy, if we do not become bearers of nonviolent attitudes and conflict resolution, if we do not stand up for disarmament, strengthen trust, practice love of enemy and commit ourselves to forgiveness, reconciliation and peace, we shall decline into insignificance.

Nonviolent Peacemaking in the Old and New Testaments

In the *Bible* we can discover a *pedagogy of peace-building* that reveals, step by step, a growing insight into the way of how to deal with and overcome *violence through the power of truth, justice and love*. It leads up to the revelation of universal love through self-giving nonviolence in Jesus. Let us look at the most important steps of this pedagogy:

a. *Roots in the Old Testament*
   The human being created in the image of God. It is important to remember the vision of humanity that is given us in Genesis 1:27: we have been created in the image of God, in the image of the Holy Trinity. To say God-in-Trinity is to say God-in-community: three divine persons, equal in dignity, who are in permanent relation with truth, justice, creativity, joy and peace, united in an infinite love which gives itself. To be created in His image therefore means: to be created as a community of men and women, tribes, nations, peoples in perfect *equality*. God wants to share with us all the aspects of his being

God-in-community; He wants the human family to live in this very relationship of Love: human beings among themselves, in relation to creation and to God.

However, we have broken and are constantly breaking this relationship of *love*, replacing it with the desire to *possess* the qualities and values of others, to dominate. This rupture with the relationship of love leads to all forms of injustice, sin, exploitation, violence, greed, killing that dominate our societies.

The *response of God,* however, to this revolt by humanity is not counter-violence. On the contrary, He replies with an act of nonviolence and love: with his *project of liberation and reconciliation.* This project shows for us the way towards the original vision of unity in love.

Israel, a small people chosen to witness in its history the way of liberation and peacemaking, is called to introduce into human history a substantially new vision, a new social concept and project, differing from the surrounding great nations. This was a demanding task for a small migrant people. In order to be able to assume this mission God sends witnesses and prophets to guide the people and He reveals himself as *Emmanuel,* which means God with the people. He promises his strength and unshakable fidelity. A profound relationship of confidence is established between Israel and Yahweh.

Violence in Israel: In contrast to the surrounding big nations, violence is no longer considered as *mythical or blind destiny,* but it becomes part of human responsibility. It is considered as a destructive force, but there is not yet a clear answer of how to conquer it in its roots. It is important to understand, however, that the *law of talion, "an eye for an eye"* (Lv 24:20), means progress of civilization over the prevailing attitude of revenge. It permits retaliation, but limits it to the same kind and degree as the injury, forbidding destruction of the adversary.

To achieve Shalom inside the people of Israel, several *demands* have to be fulfilled. The most important of these are:

> ☙ *You must adore only the unique God, the God of Justice and Love.* This contrasts the attitude of the powerful neigh-

boring nations who adored gods of power, of riches, of military strength, and attributed divine adoration to their political leaders. There should be no submission to kings and dictators.*Who are the gods* WE *adore?*

❧ *Life is sacred:* You shall not kill: to shed human blood is the gravest sin. While the surrounding pagan nations sacrificed infants to win the favor of their gods, David, for example, was not allowed to build the temple because he had shed blood.

When God renews the Covenant with Noah, he stresses only this command: life is sacred. But, as we have seen before, this law is limited to the people of Israel.

We can, however, find examples in the Old Testament that go beyond the law of talion in the direction of universal love — e.g., the four chants of the Suffering Servant of Isaiah, who resists oppression by taking upon himself all the violence in order to liberate both the people of Israel and the oppressor.

❧ Respect of *Human Rights:* a firm and permanent commitment to Human Rights is required. God manifests himself as *God of the weak*, the poor, of widows, orphans, strangers, and slaves. They must be cared for and be able to live in dignity. *This is also a precondition for peace in our own societies!*

❧ Economic and social justice: the earth is the Lord's and He wishes it to serve all, not just a few. The *Year of Jubilee*, to be celebrated once in a generation (every fifty years), was meant to give thanks to God through reciprocal pardon, reconciliation and redistribution of the goods so that everyone can live in dignity.To jubilate signifies to thank God through the acceptance of economic and social justice and reconciliation.

We find these commands in the books of Exodus and Leviticus. To sum up we can say that life in the spirit of Shalom requires *that a nation truly lives love of neighbor: it is the first level of the revelation of the Love of God.* In Jesus further dimensions of the pedagogy of peacebuilding will be revealed.

b. *Jesus' Message of Peace*

Jesus enters into human history at a moment of great violence and intense suffering for the people of Israel: Roman occupation (taxes, clashes for religious reasons, etc.); a politico-religious leadership, partly compromised with the Romans, exploiting the people with taxes and oppressive rules; an armed resistance movement, mainly in Galilee.

It is in this context that Jesus will implant the liberating, saving, healing force of *universal love* of the Father and reveal through his teaching, life, death and resurrection how to *overcome violence, injustice, all evil at its root in the conscience and heart of humans* as well as in the structures of society.

- He insists upon the absolute respect of every human person for being created by God (Jesus' parable of the good Samaritan).
- He takes the side of the downtrodden, the suffering, invigorating their own faith in order to be healed.
- He breaks through taboos: speaks to women in public, makes them messengers of the good news; he puts the care for the human person above laws (healing on the Sabbath).
- He speaks the Truth and confronts injustice freely and accepts fully the consequences of doing so (encounters with Pharisees and Sadducees, the question of the purity of the temple). He faithfully gives witness to the divine love of the Father to the very last, to the gift of his life.

In the *Sermon on the Mount,* Matthew 5 sums up the essence of Jesus' teaching. Going beyond love of neighbor, extending the pedagogy of peacemaking, Jesus reveals two further dimensions of love required for reconciling humanity in brotherhood:

1. *Love of Enemies* (Mt 5:44)

"Love your enemies, and pray for those who persecute you" has two radical, revolutionary implications:

- *Humanity is ONE*: the division between the good ones and the evil ones is over; all human life is sacred and has to be respected;

∻   *nonviolent combat to overcome evil*: Jesus cuts the spiral of violence by resisting aggression and by overcoming evil with the power of truth, justice and love. He illustrates this by taking scenes out of the life of the people: when you are slapped in the face, turn the other cheek. If they take your shirt, let them have your coat as well. This means:

- not to reply to violence with violence;
- but resist: do not accept injustice, do not remain passive, take position;
- stand up and fight with the power of truth and justice: attacking the roots of evil in the conscience of the aggressor nonviolently with respect and love;
- Believe and affirm that the adversary has a conscience that can be reached, can open, can be changed;
- This nonviolent combat aims at *overcoming the injustice and liberating the aggressor as well as the victim.* Such combat can obtain greater justice and opens the possibility of reconciliation.

2. *Self-giving Love of God*

Resistance with the power of truth and love has consequences: Jesus takes freely upon himself the violence of his adversaries, all the violence of humanity, to absorb it, to overcome it with the power of Love. This leads to his gift of life on the cross — but also to resurrection. He reveals to us the *only way* to overcome evil at its source: in the conscience of humans and humanity by taking upon us the consequences of nonviolent actions. *Thus we can create a new, reconciled relationship.*

Nonviolent combat is the realistic transforming and liberating power in human history. In the *resurrection* of Jesus, the Shalom, the renewed human person, the seed of the Kingdom of God has been implanted in our world and it continues to transform, to heal, to avoid hatred and bloodshed, to forgive and reconcile. People baptized in the name of Jesus Christ have the responsibility to work out of this perspective in their own life and in society.

Active Nonviolence Applied by Christians in Our Times: Methods and Strategies

We shall now, by way of examples, see how Christians apply this peacebuilding and liberating power of nonviolence in the present time:

Empowering the Weak and Oppressed

The women of Medellin: In a poverty-stricken barrio of Medellin, Colombia, poor people adhering to Christian base communities, by reading the Bible discover their own dignity and their responsibility to struggle against the inhuman conditions. God wants life in fullness for all. Through seminars in nonviolence they discover for themselves this power of transformation, revealed by Jesus. This helps them to overcome fear that paralyzed their energies. A process of inner and outward liberation can start. In a nonviolent campaign to obtain drinking water necessary to save the lives of their children, a group of illiterate women succeeds in touching the conscience of well-to-do women, even building solidarity with them. With this experience of their power of justice and truth, they continue the process of urbanization, *of liberation and empowerment among rich and poor.*

The peasant women of the Larzac, France: During the enlargement of a military base in the French Larzac region, 110 farmers would have had to give up their land. The nonviolent leader Lanza del Vasto takes a two weeks' fast and analyzes the situation with the peasants: should they sell their land for the military preparation of wars or resist nonviolently to preserve the soil for its original destination to produce food, to nourish people? The peasants unite and decide for nonviolent resistance, developing slowly their strategy that makes them change from conservative, politically non-committed persons to persevering, peace-workers, who defend their soil successfully during ten years of hard nonviolent combat (1972–81).

In 1973 the first mass demonstration with 60,000 participants from trade unions, peasant movements, intellectuals, church people, and students takes place in the Larzac to say NO to militarization, YES to the production of food for the hungry of the world. *A peasant woman, mother of 6 children, with little formal education gives the main speech.* The nonviolent combat has freed her from fear, liberated her hidden force of Truth, and helped her to fully develop her human and spiritual potential.

Defying Dictatorship

Madagascar 1991 and 2001: The Philippine People Power movement of 1986 had considerable impact upon countries with similar situations of oppression, such as Madagascar where the twelve years' reign of the dictator Didier Ratsiraka pushed the country into utmost poverty. In 1990, inspired by the example of the Philippines and helped by the ecumenical Justice and Peace Commission with training in nonviolence, the opposition opted for nonviolent resistance. Very well-organized weekly mass demonstrations accompanied a six-month general strike that was very costly for the poverty-stricken population.

The Christian Council of Churches of Madagascar, comprising all Christian churches of the island, and referred to as the FFKM, was accepted as mediator. It obtained a transition government, a new constitution, and elections. However, after a few years the dictator returned. When he was defeated by the elections of 2001, he refused to resign.

Several months of hard, costly nonviolent resistance and — finally — international support succeeded in bringing about the definite victory of the democratic forces. The dictator went into exile. Now the poverty-stricken country needs many years of moral and material rebuilding.

Nonviolence: Force of Healing and Pardoning

Example of *Burundi: emphatic listening between Hutus and Tutsis*:
In regions of civil war or ethnic strife, as in Burundi, church organizations are promoting *emphatic listening*, deep listening with mind and heart between small groups of Hutus and Tutsis, who have been in war over so many years.

The objective is

❞ to become able to express one's suffering;

❞ to listen to the suffering of the adversary;

❞ to overcome a one-sided view;

❞ to find common ground in the same experience of suffering; to become able to accept, to pardon, the other;

❞ to begin to act together;

❞ to overcome the origin of existing violence and injustice.

Interreligious Witness to the Sacredness of Life

Example of Lubumbashi, Democratic Republic of Congo:
Lubumbashi is the center of the copper-mining region of Katanga. Because of possibilities for work, there was a considerable influx from surrounding provinces with differing ethnic population. In the 1990s, under the dictatorship of President Mobutu, the mining industry broke down. The governor decided to get rid of the immigrants.

Ethnic hatred followed and, after unrest at the university, *ethnic massacres* were threatening. The nonviolent movement GANVE (founded in 1989 by Jean Goss) approached *Christian and Muslim religious leaders*. A public interreligious peace prayer with thousands of participants was organized during which the religious authorities affirmed together: God, Allah, is the creator of all human beings. He protects all of them and demands safeguard and dignity for each person. Encouraged by this moral support, a nonviolent action was started: people of both ethnic groups, suffering starvation because of unemployment, began *together* to plant vegetables in empty spaces near the city. Through this life-supporting work they discovered their common needs as human beings. Hatred was overcome through solidarity and new reconciled relationships could evolve.

Similar large-scale public prayer and fasting of Christians and Muslims with their leaders recently took place in *Ivory Coast* to avoid the atrocities of a civil war.

The efforts for a peaceful solution of the Iraq crisis are presently strongly supported by Christians, their churches and religious bodies in particular in the USA, in Europe, and by the Vatican, the Orthodox, and the World Council of Churches.

Finally, all depends upon our own conversion to believe in the transforming power of nonviolence as Gods's way to peace and that we apply it in our own life and acting. Whether or not we see an immediate result, we should remember that nothing is ever lost that is done out of the power of love. It will bear fruit one day.

(Peace Day, Catholic University Leuven, Belgium
Lecture by Hildegard Goss-Mayr, February 20, 2003)

Prospects for the Future

Was it then all in vain? This sobering and demanding question which, at the outbreak of the Gulf War, threw my husband Jean into deep depression, I ask myself, too. So do many who have been active in peace work for years. Is not violence growing around us, within us, in marriage and partnership, with children and youth, in our society that has become egoistic, individualistic, and hardened? Ethnic and national tensions, particularly since the downfall of "communism," lead to new wars that hurt primarily the civilian population.

But our view must take on a wider perspective. Since the transition in Eastern Europe, the neo-liberal capitalist economic system has gained dominance over the world. Its aim is profit and power. Humankind must serve it. In the face of brutal competition, small ones fall by the wayside: employers and employees, workers and farmers. The weak and underqualified are exploited or marginalized, excluded. Without work or shelter, hungry, ill, discarded, millions and millions of people subsist in misery.

This dominant economic system is only one characteristic of the new epoch we have entered: the epoch of global society, in which humankind forms a single entity. This creates a unique chance, as well as a frightening temptation to totalitarianism. Which will it be? An open, democratic world community, or the dictates of a centralized economic, political, and military power, steered by a manipulated media? Neither one nor the other is going to prevail in its totality. But in view of the concentrated power of anti-human forces, the challenge takes on a new dimension. Facing it will require an efficient, globally coordinated network of persons working for justice, peace, and a life of dignity. Our struggle that is dominated by the power of love will have to be led even more insistently, doggedly, devotedly.

We should not underestimate the subversive, revolutionary, and at the same time liberating and healing power of nonviolence. Has not the peace work of the last fifty years shown what this power can do when persons join together and start to act in solidarity? Has truth not shown itself as the power of the poor? Are not peaceful solutions being intensely looked for — yes, even striven for — precisely in places where deadly violence is escalating?

In this new situation we are all on our way, seeking perspectives and priorities; we are searching for the work of God's Spirit as present in our time, God's will for us now. Against this background, I now want to point out several perspectives that presently appear to me to be essential. Perhaps they will show the way for peace work in the future.

Human unity — a positive challenge

It appears to me fundamental that we recognize and welcome the present development toward human unity. It is already having an effect in economy, politics, and technology, in the media and in certain cultural areas, under positive as well as negative circumstances. However it progresses much more slowly, painfully, and hesitantly in human feelings and insights and in the spiritual and religious area. Many fear, consciously or unconsciously, to lose their own identity, their own way of being, culture, or religion. This is one of the important causes of the new nationalism and religious fundamentalism. Thus building up confidence in both oneself and the Other — in manifold ways, at all levels of life — becomes a basic necessity. Whoever recognizes and affirms the beauty and depth of his or her own culture, way of being, and religion, and feels steadfast in it, will become free and ready to experience the beauty and depth of others. Interaction with the Other is then not a menace, but an enrichment. When we reach this state, we will be able to recognize the revelation of God in others and to accept the gift of their truth.

Only then is it possible to experience unity within diversity as joyful. Only then will we be able to give others their due respect, to invest our energies in the realization of their basic rights, and to accept sharing in justice. Only then will we begin to cooperate, step by step, in working together on a global project that has the human family at its center. That project will have the aim of establishing a new social order, building up a responsible relationship with resources, the biosphere, and the cosmos — all this through democratic attitudes and the methods of nonviolence. Utopia? Yes! Because only a person with unequivocal aims, who bears in herself the image of a united, brotherly world — a likeness of the triune God — and believes in it, will find the strength to start upon the toilsome path of drawing nearer to this Utopia, to the realm of God in this world. She will seek and pursue it because in it lies the salvation of humanity.

The coming together of the religions and their peace mission

The new situation leads, of necessity, to an encounter of religions. Indeed, this is already taking place. Many react with fearful rejection, with fundamentalist attitudes, in the Christian churches as well as in Islam, in Jewry and also in Asian religions. This attitude is propagated and abused, mostly by political groups. However, the way into the future by no means lies in syncretism, in the mixing of religions. On the contrary, a return to the deepest roots of our beliefs is required, to the original inspiration. If we realize these values honestly in our life and actions, then we shall find the freedom to meet and engage in dialogue with persons of different belief. Only in this way can we discover those values, which are common to us as believers and that are required by the world for a humane togetherness.

Out of these encounters should emanate a common witness of believers and cooperation in the absolute respect of individuals, even of the enemy. They should produce a clear taking of sides for nonviolence, the protection of basic rights, and the social good of all, in particular of the poor and of minorities. The degree to which it is possible to move world religions toward such concrete responsibility will be decisive for the direction our humanity project will take.

Christians must return to the Sermon on the Mount and place themselves clearly and consistently on the side of the poor and the excluded, demanding that their rights be respected in politics and the economy. People of faith must become pioneers, bearers of nonviolent attitudes and conflict resolution everywhere. We must strengthen trust, forgiveness, reconciliation, and peace. If we do not, we will decline into insignificance and the Angel of our Churches will remove our candlestick, as did the Angel of the Church of Ephesus (Acts 2:5). Even worse, we will betray the clear command to be witnesses of God's revolutionary love. Yet on all continents Christian groups have risen, sometimes with great sacrifice, and become active in this spirit. May their testimony awaken many and bring them to solidarity!

Against this background, there results a new concrete task for the peace movement: training in nonviolence for peace services. This is beginning to be recognized too.

A project for humankind demands the efficient, worldwide coordination of instruments for nonviolent conflict resolution, for the prevention of violence, for forgiveness and reconciliation. In the past fifty years, from Gandhi to "People Power" in the Philippines and the "Velvet Revolution" in Eastern Europe, people have been experimenting with this liberating and healing power. Now what is needed is to train a great number of competent, experienced women and men committed to nonviolence for the resolution of problems — in partnerships, among children and youth, in our social conflicts, as well as in ethnic, national, and international situations of violence. These persons should be ready to do peace work wherever it is necessary, voluntarily accepting all the consequences and risks involved. We already have models in certain denominational and civilian peace services, such as Peace Brigades International, the Ecumenical Peace Service in Germany, or those within the framework of IFOR. Peace research institutes and universities also offer training.

As yet, we are far too few to be able to offer peace troops to town administrations, governments, and international institutions. However, a beginning has been made. The limited actions taken to try the power of this movement are increasing. On the basis of nonviolent peace services, we will be able to demand disarmament more convincingly than ever. The shift from armed conflicts will seem more feasible.

The media as channels of hope

We are much aware of the dominant role of the media in forming world opinion. No doubt this will only increase with time. Their diabolic potential has already shown itself — for example, during the Gulf war or in Rwanda. In this mode, only the sensational is deserving of coverage. We are overwhelmed by pictures and stories of violence that discourage us or deaden our senses.

But the media also have a magnificent chance to be bearers of hope. During my many years of experience, I have seen again and again how people in situations of psychological and material calamity, of violence and war, need to be presented with the whole truth. On the one hand, this means recognizing injustice and suffering in its whole depth and structure. On the other hand, it means confronting those forces that overcome injustice, that can lead out of a crisis. We need concrete examples of the power of testimony present in the truth. We need humane, compassionate help to regain confidence in the good in ourselves, to discover our self-esteem, and to find the strength to stand up and become active. Publications, radio, and film, as well as TV, can and must become powerful, influential carriers of peace messages. They are the natural pedagogues for nonviolent peacemaking.

We must consider and analyze many further perspectives, finding more solutions through the power of nonviolence. For example, the struggle for genuine partnership between the genders is one of the biggest challenges engaging humanity at present: we cannot neglect it. Neither can we neglect the attempt to protect the environment, the living space of all creation; the protection of the human element in genetic research, in the transference of life, and dying in dignity; the termination of nuclear technology with its potential of uncontrollable destruction; the flagrant injustice of North-South relations ... the list goes on.

Great hopes, great threats lie ahead of us. But we can work with confidence on our humanity project because we know that we are part of the project of God's love for humanity, launched before time began. For these new steps on the path to the realm of God, we know we are being borne up by the living Spirit of the Lord. If we open up to God unconditionally in firm and unalterable faith, then it will be possible for us, through that power, to mirror God's love project in our humanity project.

God has called us to this shaping of the world from the power of truth and love and has endowed us with His spirit. May we, in full awareness of this task, proceed hopefully, like Hildegard of Bingen:

> Humanity stands at the center of the structure of the world.
> Although small in stature, humanity is powerful through the
>   power of its soul. It can set into movement the higher and
>   the lower things.
> Whatever it does with its right or left hand, it penetrates the
> universe, because, in the strength of the inner person, it
>   carries the ability, to do such things.
> The power of the soul encompasses the entire world.

(This article is adapted from Goss-Mayrs' book, *Wie Feinde Freunde Werden* [Herder 1996]. It appeared in *Fellowship* [May/June, 2002], pp. 4-6)

Chronology of
Hildegard Goss-Mayr

January 22, 1930	Born to Kaspar and Erika Mayr in Vienna, Austria, the fourth of five children
1937–45	Experienced persecution under Nazi regime
1946–53	University education in Vienna and New Haven (USA): philosophy, philology and history
1953	PhD from the University of Vienna: "*sub auspiciis praesidentis*" (gold medal), the first time this highest degree of the University of Vienna was awarded to a woman
1953– early 1960s	Traveling secretary for the International Fellowship of Reconciliation with priority on East-West dialogue
1958	Married to Jean Goss; they begin work together for international peace and justice
	Work in Prague and Moscow including organization of the first international meeting of the Catholic, Protestant and Orthodox churches on evangelical non-violence
1959	Work in Hungary, Poland, Czechoslovakia, and the United States
1960	Birth of twins, Myriam and Etienne
	Work in Romania, Bulgaria, and Yugoslavia
1962	Work in Latin America
	Collaboration on many proposals to Second Vatican Council concerning gospel-based alternatives to violence, exploitation and war, as expressed in the Council documents *Gaudium et Spes*. In Rome, worked with Dom Hélder Câmara, Karl Rahner, Yves Congar and Bernard Häring

1963	Work in Britain, Ireland, Scandinavia, Portugal and Spain
1964–65	Family stays one year in Brazil
	First nonviolence groups in Latin America founded
1967	Uruguay: first international meeting on revolutionary nonviolence; nineteen countries represented
	Brazil: first official national seminar on revolutionary nonviolence
1968	Vienna: second theological conference of the Catholic, Protestant and Orthodox churches from east and west on evangelical noviolence
	Work with leading Latin American bishops including Dom Hélder Câmara, Dom Alois Lorscheider, and Mons. Leonidas Proaño
	Work in Prague
1970–71	Family stays one year in Mexico
	Work in Colombia, Venezuela, Chile, Argentina, the United States and Portugal
1972	Work in Spain, Portugal, Scandinavia and the Balkans
1973	Work in Angola, Mozambique and South Africa
1974	Work in Mozambique, Angola and Portugal
	Second coordinating conference of movements in Medellin (Colombia).
	Efforts in Latin America over the years culminate in the emergence of a continental network of cooperation of nonviolent groups "Servicio Paz y Justicia" (Nonviolent Service for Peace and Justice in Latin America — SERPAJ-AL)
1974–75	Work in Lebanon
1976	Work in Israel, South Africa, Rhodesia and Tanzania
	With Jean Goss, recipient of Luis Maria Xirinacs Award from Pax Christi, Spain
1977	Bogotá: Seminar for Latin American Bishops on "Nonviolence: the Liberating Force of the Gospel"; proposals elaborated for the Continental Bishops' Conference at Puebla

1979	Work in Salvador
	With Jean Goss, recipient of Award for Commitment to Human Rights, Work from the Doctor Bruno Kreisky Foundation, Austria.
	With Jean Goss, nominated by Quaker Peace Service for the Nobel Peace Prize
1980	Work in Lebanon
1981–82	Work in Poland
1982	As vice-president of the International Fellowship of Reconciliation, addressed the Second United Nations Special Session on Disarmament
1984	Work in the Philippines; seminars helped lay the foundation for the nonviolent overthrow of the Marcos regime
	Participation in the "Peace Decade" in the German Democratic Republic
1985	Work in Nicaragua, including helping in the formation of Serpaj-Nicaragua
1985–88	Extensive work in Asia, especially in Thailand, Bangladesh, and the Philippines
	Numerous seminars in many countries in Europe
1986	With Jean Goss, recipient of the Pax Christi USA Pope Paul VI "Teacher for Peace" award
1987	Work in Ecuador
	With Jean Goss, nominated by Mairead Maguire for the Nobel Peace Prize
1988	Michigan, US: Honorary Doctor of Divinity degree, Kalamazoo College
	Work in Hong Kong
	With Jean Goss, selected as Honorary President of the International Fellowship of Reconciliation
1989	Special counsel to the European Ecumenical Assembly on Peace, Justice, and the Integrity of Creation, May 1987, Basel, Switzerland
	Seminars in South Korea and Hong Kong with Richard Deats

1991	(April) As they prepare for work in Madagascar to overcome the dictatorship of Pres. Ratsiraka, Jean Goss dies
	(May) Recipient of Niwano Peace Prize in Tokyo, Japan
	(November) Work in Madagascar
1992	(February) Seminars in Ivory Coast on nonviolence with Alfred Bour, FOR-France
	Seminars in Austria, Switzerland and France
	Co-recipient with Diana Francis of the Pfeffer Peace Prize
	(August/September) Seminars in Brazzaville, Congo with Christian Renoux, FOR-France
1993	Seminars in France, Austria and East Germany (Kottbus, Dresden)
	(January/February) Work on crisis resolution in Rwanda and East Zaire (Goma, Bukavu) with B. Eliat of Belgium
	(October) International Colloquium honoring Jean Goss in Paris
	(November/December) Work in Madagascar with Alfred Bour
	In Rwanda, dramatic situation preceding genocide
1994	Work in France, Germany (Tibet Parliament), Austria, and Italy
	(October) Seminars in N'Djamena, Chad (Tchad Nonviolence) with Alfred Bour
1995	(December) Invited to Burundi by Bishop's Conference and CRID, with Jean-Denis Renaud, FOR-Suisse-Romande
	Seminars in Germany, France, Austria and Rome (International Session for Religious)
1996	(March) Burundi: Seminars with Alfred Bour
	Work with FOR in Wales, Germany, and Austria
	(May) Bangladesh: Seminar on democracy preceding elections
	(August) Sweden: IFOR-Council on nonviolence in different religious traditions

1997	Vienna: Lenten sermons on Reconciliation Work in Germany, Switzerland, France
	(February) Work in Zagreb, Croatia, with Ana and Otto Raffai to build a network of peace groups
	(May) Visit to Japan for Niwano Peace Foundation
	(October) Burundi: seminars and coordination of peace groups
1998	Work in France, Austria, Switzerland, Germany and Italy (Rimini)
	(July/August) Burundi: seminars Kenya: Work with refugees from Rwanda
	(November) Togo: Eglise Presbyterienne, with Christian Renoux
1999	Work in Italy, France, Switzerland and Germany
2000	Work in France, Belgium, Germany and Austria
	(September) Work in Poland
	(October) Lubumbashi, Democratic Republic of the Congo: visit and support for GANVE nonviolent group
2001	(January) Italy: Seminars in Alba and Rimini (John XXIII Association)
	(February) Florence: Interethnic conference on Kosovo
	(August) Israel/Palestine: Intifada, preparation of Peace Pilgrimage
2002	Israel/Palestine:
	(February and April) Height of Intifada 2, Peace Pilgrimage to support peace groups in Israel and Palestine
	(July) USA: IFOR Council and Address to AFOR
2003	Belgium: Lecture at Peace Day of University of Leuven la Neuve
	(March) Austria: Accompanying Israeli/Palestinian peace delegation
	(June) Berlin: Speech at Ecumenical Kirchentag
	(September) Vorarlberg, Austria: Celebrating fifty years of FOR-Austria and 50 years of FOR service of

H. Goss-Mayr (with Nobel Peace Laureates Adolfo Perez Esquivel and Mairead Corrigan Maguire)

(October) Japan: International Peace Forum of Niwano Peace Foundation

2004   (February) Interview: *Friedenstreiberinnen* ("Relentless Promoters of Peace") by Ute Scheub
Lectures on Terrorism and Seminar on Sermon on the Mount, L'Arche France. Work in Südtirol, Italy and lecture tour in Palermo, Sicily

2005   (January) Corrardi, Italy: Interview for doctoral dissertation on nonviolence

(July) Schlaining, Austria: Seminar at International Peace Research Institute

(November) University of Graz, Austria: Lecture on Thomas Merton's contribution to peace theology (with Jim Forest)

(December) Schalomdiakonat, Germany: Christian/ Muslim Seminar on peace

2006   Lectures in Germany and Austria

(March) Brussels, Belgium: Speech at inauguration of "Sortir de la Violence"

(May) Philippines: Seminars on Peace Building and Reconciliation marking the twentieth anniversary of People Power Revolution

(August) Speech at FOR-Austria Youth Camp with youth from Eastern Europe and Turkey

(December) Lecture tour in Switzerland

Works Cited

Brittain, Vera. *The Rebel Passion. A Short History of Some Pioneer Peace-Makers.* Nyack, NY: Fellowship Publications, 1964.

Dear, John, S.J. Interview with Hildegard Goss-Mayr (Unpublished, 1986).

Deats, Richard. "Jean Goss, Combative Mystic." *Fellowship* (March/April 1994): 13.

Easwaran, Eknath, *A Man to Match His Mountains: Badshah Khan, Nonviolent Soldier of Islam.* Petaluma, CA: Nilgiri Press, 1985.

Egan, Eileen. *Peace Be With You. Justified Warfare or the Way of Nonviolence.* Maryknoll, NY: Orbis Books, 1999.

Forest, Jim and Nancy. *Four Days in February: The Story of the Nonviolent Overthrow of the Marcos Regime.* Basingstoke, UK: Marshall Pickering, 1988.

Franklin, James L. "A prelate explains 'revolution of love.' " *Boston Globe* (1 June 1986) 81, 84.

Goss-Mayr, Jean and Hildegard. *The Gospel and the Struggle for Justice and Peace. Training Seminar in Evangelical Nonviolence and Methods of Engaging in It.* Translated from the French by Dave Parry. Stockholm: The Swedish Ecumenical Council and the International Fellowship of Reconciliation, 1990.

Goss-Mayr, Hildegard. Address to United Nations General Assembly, 25 June 1988. Unpublished document.

_____. *Der Mensch vor dem Unrecht. Spiritualität und Praxis — Gewaltlose Befreiung.* Vienna: Europaverlag, 1976.

_____. *Die Macht der Gewalt-Losen: Der Christ und die Revolution am Beispiel Braziliens.* Graz, Austria: Verlag Styria, 1968.

_____. "Prospects for the Future." *Fellowship* (May/June 2002): 5-6.

_____. *Wie Feinde Freunde Werden.* Freiburg: Herder, 1996.

_____. "When Prayer and Revolution Became People Power." *Fellowship* (March 1987): 8-11.

Houver, Gerard. *A Non-Violent Lifestyle: Conversations with Jean and Hildegard Goss-Mayr*. Translated by Richard Bateman. London: Lamp Press, 1981.

King, Mary. *Mahatma Gandhi and Martin Luther King, Jr.: The Power of Nonviolent Action*. Paris: Cultures of Peace Series, UNESCO Publishing, 1999.

Kurtz, Lester R. "Natural-born Activist: Hildegard Goss-Mayr." *Peace Review* 13 (3) 2001: 457-461.

Lester, Muriel. "Tale from Vienna." *Fellowship* (January 1950): 17-18.

Mayr, Richard. *Diary and letters, tr. and ed. by Lilian Stevenson from a memoir by his father, Kaspar Mayr*. London: Lutterworth Press, 1947.

Pope Paul VI. *Gaudium et Spes:* Pastoral Constitution on the Church in the Modern World. http://www.vatican.va/archive/hist_councils/ii_vatican_council/documents/vat-ii_cons_19651207_gaudium-et-spes_en.html (Accessed 25 February 2008).

Schell, Jonathan. *The Unconquerable World. Power, Nonviolence, and The Will of the People*. New York: Henry Holt and Company, Metropolitan Books, 2003.

Shannon, William H., Ed. *Witness to Freedom: The Letters of Thomas Merton in Times of Crises*. New York: Farrar, Straus, Giroux, 1994.

Articles ▪ *Reports* ▪ *Talks*

Unless otherwise noted, Hildegard Goss-Mayr is the author of the articles, talks and reports. A question mark (?) indicates that the date of the entry is unknown.

Absolute Respect for the Human Being. Reconciliation International (February 1991).

Alagamar: Nonviolent Land Struggle, IFOR Report (July 1980).

Christians and Peace. English and Russian. 3a. (January 1, 1958).

Christmas Letters. German and English (1976, 1977, 1979, 1981, 1982, 1983, 1986, 1988, 1990, 1992).

Choosing Means Toward a Just End, *Fellowship* (October/November 1983).

Confidential. Work in Jordan, Jean and Hildegard Goss-Mayr (May 1987).

Confidential. Work in the Philippines (February 7 to 29, 1984).

File of letters from Hildegard Goss-Mayr to Richard Deats.

File of letters from Richard Deats to Hildegard Goss-Mayr.

IFOR Documents on International Day for Justice & Peace in Central America. January 12-13, 1980 (coordinated by Jean and Hildegard Goss-Mayr, July 24, 1979).

Internal Memo. Contact visit to Zagreb, Croatia (March 23 to 27, 1992)

Jean Goss 1912-1991. Cahiers de Reconciliation No. 4 (special issue,1991).

Jean Goss, Combative Mystic. Jean Goss Colloquium and Seminar in Paris, France, by Richard Deats. *Fellowship* (March/April 1994).

Jean Goss. Seminar/Colloquium, Paris (October 30 to November 1, 1992).

Letter to Archbishop McGrath & Archbishop Obando y Brava. Madagascar *Cahiers de la Reconciliation No. 2* (special issue, 1995).

Marked for Life. An Interview. Reconciliation International (November 1988).

Messengers of Nonviolence, by Robert Ellsberg, *Catholic Worker* (September 1986).

A Model for Peaceful Transition to Democracy in Africa. Brazzaville Seminars in Congo (August 23 to September 6, 1992).

Nonviolence is the Atomic Bomb of the People. Peace by Peace (March 1987).

Nonviolent Seminar in Negros (June 1988).

Overcoming Wartime Enmity, *Fellowship* (September/October 1994).

Peace Profile: Goss-Mayr. Signs of Hope, *Fellowship* (1980).

Puebla: A Step Forward, IFOR Report (?)

Risks and Promises on the Way to Becoming Peace Church. Reconciliation International (April 1987).

Seeds of Nonviolence in Lebanon, Jean Goss. Reconciliation International (?)

Seminar in Chad, Hildegard Goss-Mayr & Alfred Bour (October 23 to November 6, 1994).

Seminar in Rwanda and East of Zaire. Hildegard Goss-Mayr and Bruno Eliot (Confidential) (January 21 to February 8, 1993).

Seminar on Nonviolence in Bangladesh (January 26 to February 5, 1986).

Seminars on Active Nonviolence in the Philippines (June 19 to July 12, 1984).

Statement of IFOR to the Second Special Session on Disarmament (1982).

The Crossroads at Puebla, Jean and Hildegard Goss-Mayr. IFOR Report (?)

Transforming Power of Nonviolence by the Philippine People. Talk at Groton, Massachusetts (April 5, 1986).

A Visit to Nicaragua, Reconciliation International (February 1986).

Visit to Poland (April 19 to 30, 1989).

With Peacemakers in Wartime Israel, Hildegard Goss-Mayr and Jim Forest. IFOR Report (October 1982).

Work in the German Democratic Republic (January 11 to 16, 1990).

Work in Ivory Coast (February 3 to 17, 1992).

Work with Nonviolent Groups in Asia (April 2 to 29, 1988).